Inspiring
Greatness

A Community's Commitment to a Brighter Future

The Independence, Missouri School District
Board of Education, and Superintendent, Dr. Jim Hinson

Note: The term "Western Independence" throughout this book refers to the west-ernmost neighborhoods within the city limits of Independence, Missouri.

Table
of Contents

Dedication

In August 2008, the Independence School District began classes in six additional schools, with more than 2,600 additional students, annexed from the Kansas City School District after a two-year struggle to change the boundary that had divided the two districts for more than 50 years. No other school district in America has ever achieved an annexation of the scale and scope accomplished in Independence, the city where Harry S. Truman, 33rd President of the United States, grew up.

This book is dedicated to the students, faculty, staff, patrons and friends of the Independence School District and to residents of Independence and Sugar Creek, Missouri, who displayed extraordinary faith and courage to change the destiny of their children and their schools for the better.

With passionate displays of grassroots cooperation, thousands of people volunteered as members of neighborhood groups, church congregations, civic associations and simply as committed individuals to achieve a goal that history had denied them for decades.

Annexation from the Kansas City School District – thought impossible by many observers – was achieved through a challenging, complex process hampered by Missouri state statutes that denied school boundary change, lawsuits, lockouts, accusations, non-stop media scrutiny and formidable resistance by the Kansas City School District and its attorneys.

Through it all, residents of Western Independence and the neighboring city of Sugar Creek met every challenge with conviction, hard work, sweat, prayers and persistence. They persevered and ultimately prevailed, celebrating victory in their community with an inspiring "Extreme School Makeover" to renew the annexed schools which, today, are thriving and providing new hope for parents, students and the community.

Inspiring Greatness is not only the motto of the Independence School District; it is the legacy of those people, young and old, rich and poor, who dedicated their time and talents to realize their dream of creating a brighter future for their schools and generations of children to come.

Inspiring Greatness is dedicated to those people with sincere appreciation. All proceeds from the sale of this book are donated to the School District of Independence Foundation, which provides funding for programs, scholarships, and outreach services in order to expand and enhance educational opportunities for students.

The Board of Education
Independence School District
Dr. Jim Hinson, Superintendent
March 2010

Foreword

A strong public education system has been one of the crowning achievements of the American experiment. However, for decades the mass exodus from the urban core has devastated some of our cities. Families with resources left the city and withdrew their children from the public system. The result was a long and painful demise of our public education system. The hardest hit were urban schools which became the schools of last resort for low-income families who had few options. National pride in our public educational system turned to national embarrassment.

The attempts to fix the ailing system have been many and varied. The results have been largely disappointing. One effort stands out among the rest as an inspiring example of what creative, committed educators, with the support of their community, can accomplish. *Inspiring Greatness* is the amazing story of how committed citizens took on the daunting challenge of transforming their troubled school system into one of the nation's finest. With vision and determination, the leadership of the communities of Sugar Creek and Independence, Missouri, faced the difficult realities of their urban environment, marshaled the political, religious and business forces to their cause, and produced a stunning example for the nation of how public schools can be the catalyst to restore vitality to a community.

When educated parents choose to relocate in declined areas of a city, largely because of the excellence of the schools that serve those communities, the future for that city is indeed an optimistic one. Quality education is key to the resurgence of new life in our nation's cities. *Inspiring Greatness* is a carefully chronicled blueprint of how one urban school system has ignited energy and imagination for the redevelopment of their city. It is a hopeful model we have long awaited.

Robert Lupton, PhD
President – Focused Community Strategies
Atlanta, Georgia

Introduction

Harry S. Truman graduated from Independence High School, now known as William Chrisman High School, in 1901.

Fond of reading history, he compiled a near-perfect attendance record and consistently scored high marks. He would later write, "I do not remember a bad teacher in all my experiences."

His bronze statue now rises outside the old Jackson County Courthouse near the home where he lived with his wife Bess before he was elected an administrative judge for the Eastern District of Jackson County in 1922, beginning his political life seven miles from Kansas City.

After leaving public office in 1952, Mr. Truman retired to Independence and lived with Bess on Delaware Avenue until his death in 1972. Every morning until his last years, the former president dressed in a neatly pressed suit, pinched a knot in a necktie, laced up his shoes tightly and then dropped a hat squarely on his head to embark on a two-mile walk through his neighborhood. School children who saw him timed his pace at exactly 120 steps per minute.

With a population of 111,500 and a proud pioneering legacy, Independence is Missouri's fourth-largest city, a magnet for light manufacturing companies, their employees and families.

The Independence School District was established in 1866. Yet, in the 1970s, issues in the Kansas City School District began to erode civic optimism and thwart economic development in Western Independence and the adjacent city of Sugar Creek, where the Kansas City School District operated seven schools.

The Kansas City School District was in financial distress. Considered one of the nation's finest urban school districts in the 1950s and 1960s, by the 1970s some of its schools and programs were suffering. As noted by education writer Paul Ciotti in an article published by The Cato Institute, between 1969 and 1989 Kansas City School District voters failed to approve a tax increase 19 times. Test scores dropped. Teachers' morale slumped. In the 1990s, conditions at its schools in Western Independence and Sugar Creek began to seriously decline.[1]

Perhaps most disconcerting of all, the drop-out rate in Western Independence schools soared. In Van Horn High School's 1974 yearbook 521 seniors were pictured. In 1998, 83 seniors were pictured. Parents grew increasingly upset about the quality of education their children received in the Kansas City School District. Young families stopped moving to the neighborhoods. Houses became vacant or were converted to transient rental properties. Businesses closed. The area suffered from high crime and economic misery. Neighborhood self-esteem hit an all-time low.

Western Independence and Sugar Creek soon became a battleground for many residents; the Kansas City School District their adversary. The goal: to reclaim their local schools, rebuild dreams of prosperity and create new hope for their children's future.

Dr. Jim Hinson, Superintendent of the Independence School District, stepped forward as one of several concerned civic leaders who began working to fuel the community's faith that it could achieve change for the better. In inspiring displays of cooperation, passion and commitment, people in all walks of life across the community rallied to fight for school annexation. *Inspiring Greatness* tells their story.

——————————

1

The Forum for Change

"Let our people go!"

Paul Wrabec, Resident of Sugar Creek

On February 9, 2006, a Thursday, red neon lights at the Englewood Theatre lit the cold early evening as more than 800 people jammed past the box office into the lobby and down the aisles to fill every seat and line the interior walls. Outside, another 200 lined up trying to get in.

Carrying microphones and recording gear, radio station reporters brushed against videographers with portable spotlights. Edgy reporters from local TV stations and newspapers created a scene that seemed to anticipate the arrival of a movie star or famous rock band.

The event was a public forum organized by a nonprofit community group, Progress Independence, to discuss a pending Missouri senate bill that would establish procedures for annexing Kansas City schools into the Independence School District. Dr. Jim Hinson, Superintendent of the Independence School District, Missouri State Senator Victor Callahan and Dr. Bernard Taylor, Superintendent of the Kansas City School District, would address the issue of a potential school boundary change and answer questions from the audience.

The widely anticipated event was a magnet for pent-up frustration and disappointment many taxpayers in Western Independence and adjacent Sugar Creek had felt for years. It attracted grandmothers in their 80s and young mothers with babies on their hips. It drew fathers of school children, men who ordinarily would not leave their house after a long day's work, but who showed up in their overalls and t-shirts. It engaged teachers and students from both school districts concerned about what the future might hold for their schools.

In the lobby, a group of Independence police officers stood watch. Outside, squad cars reflected wavy red lines from the theatre's neon marquee. A truck from the Independence Fire Department idled a block from the theatre in case of emergency.

The evening's moderator, Chris Adams, Director of Debate for Truman High School in the Independence School District, approached the lectern in front of the curtained movie screen and brought the forum to order. Hinson, Callahan and Taylor sat facing the audience on the stage behind two, long folding tables, ready to address the issue of potential school boundary change and answer questions from the audience.

Taylor, on the left, and Hinson, in the middle, were dressed almost identically in blue shirts, dark neckties and dark suits. Callahan, on the right, wore a white shirt, a sea-blue necktie and a black, double-breasted suit on his tall frame. All three waited quietly for the forum to begin.

Independence Mayor Ron Stewart stood to make brief remarks, urging the audience to "keep calm." He knew the school district issues were emotional for many present. "We apologize for not being able to accommodate everyone. Obviously," he said to the noisy crowd, "the concern here is even bigger than we thought." To that remark the throng responded with applause and loud cheers.

Eileen Weir, co-founder of Progress Independence, who would later refer to the forum as "a mob scene," spoke next. She told the gathering that night, "We will answer as many questions and comments as possible," noting that each of the three featured speakers would have a few minutes for opening statements. She introduced Senator Callahan first. He was out of his chair and at stage front with a microphone in his hand as fast as a runner trying to steal second base in a decisive baseball game.

"The history of the Kansas City School District has been a tragic one," the senator declared. "It is filled with chapters of incompetence and mismanagement, chapters of the abuse of taxpayers' dollars, chapters of lawsuits and chapters of poor education. We are here to talk about the future."

The audience exploded into cheers. The senator recounted results of a task force he had created to study the issue, and outlined challenges the community faced. As he explained potential ways that, politically and legally, the school boundary line might be changed, he was interrupted by frequent ovations.

"I want to give you the power as taxpayers to set your course!" he exhorted, generating whoops from the crowd. Turning left and right to address every corner of the theatre, Callahan was obviously fired up—and so was the crowd, heads nodding in agreement with his passionate oratory.

More than once, Adams interrupted Callahan from the lectern to calm the audience with reminders for all to be quiet or she would stop the forum. Yet repeatedly people cheered and clapped without hesitation after waiting years for the discourse now finally taking place before their eyes.

If one milestone occasion exposed discordant issues between the Independence and Kansas City School Districts, linking the past with the future of public education in Western Independence, the forum at the Englewood Theater was it. Nothing like it had ever occurred in the community.

Live and in color, the Western Independence school boundary issue was finally going mainstream. Taped for the ten o'clock news and local cable TV, the forum was not advertised as a "debate." Yet many people would go home thinking that the Independence School District and its patrons had much to gain, while the Kansas City School District had much to lose.

The forum was a catalyst for information and opinions that most people there obviously wanted to hear and to share, and which neither Taylor nor Hinson had addressed publicly in detail until then. Both Taylor and Hinson learned a great deal about their districts' citizens that night.

As Hinson would say later, "The number of individuals that showed up that night at the theatre—those who could *get in* to the theater—and the passion with which they addressed the situation, *attacking* the situation in some circumstances, was very revealing. I was not aware that so many people in the community really wanted a change.

"I knew there were individuals who were very passionate about it. But to see that number of people, to see the faces of the parents and kids who were there made me understand there was a large group of individuals, not just some, who were very passionate and might do whatever it would take to make this change happen."

For Taylor the forum experience was illuminating, though perhaps not so rewarding as it was for Hinson. When Taylor, from the stage, said "I know there has been a history with the Kansas City School District and that some of you are not pleased with that history," some in the crowd hooted and laughed.

Photo courtesy of *The Examiner.*

Hundreds of citizens jammed a public forum on February 9, 2006 to discuss a proposed Missouri senate bill that would establish procedures for annexing Kansas City schools into the Independence School District. Dr. Jim Hinson, Superintendent of the Independence School District, addresses the crowd as Dr. Bernard Taylor, then-Superintendent of the Kansas City School District, and State Senator Victor Callahan, at right, listen intently.

Weir later would say, "Bernard Taylor really was quite impressive...He maintained his demeanor throughout the whole thing...Those people were furious at the way that they had been treated by the Kansas City School District all those years."

Weir also was concerned about their obvious bias against the Kansas City School District because "there were some fine teachers doing good jobs in those schools and, you know, they were kind of being caught up into all the negativity."

In his remarks and responses to audience questions, Taylor explained how a federal de-segregation case in which the Kansas City School District had been embroiled for years had mandated many circumstances for the district over which it had no control. "We do have some problems," he acknowledged, "but these problems are the same problems that many school districts across the country are experiencing."

He noted that the Kansas City School District had been released from the de-segregation case by the courts in 1999 and was working to change things for the better, in many cases successfully. "There are a lot of unanswered questions," he admitted. "Are there challenges for the Kansas City School District? Yes, there are." With that, some in the crowd jeered him.

In fact, in the 1960s and early 70s, the Kansas City School District had been a model for urban districts across the nation. It managed many outstanding programs for its students in the early 21st century. Taylor discussed some of the district's educational initiatives and success stories. Unfortunately, he was speaking to the wrong crowd. While some supporters of the Kansas City School District were seated in the theatre, most people there were not. Many lambasted the Kansas City School District for poor performance, making Taylor a target, often prompting him into defensive remarks.

Progress Independence had distributed numbered slips of paper to people who entered the forum. Moderator Adams called out numbers from the stage. One by one, people were given a microphone as they approached the stage to ask their questions.

Some did not ask questions but instead used the opportunity to express fervent complaints. For example, one woman described the Kansas City schools in Western Independence as a "no man's land." Another noted that two of her children attended Van Horn High but that, in her opinion, "their diplomas aren't going to be worth anything" because of the school's poor performance record. A third accused the Kansas City School District of operating schools where children "get lost in the system." Another, citing the Kansas City School District's operating budget, said, "I don't see where this money is being spent" in Western Independence schools.

Paul Wrabec, a landlord in Sugar Creek, told Taylor that he received $200 per month less for houses that he rented in the Kansas City School District compared to rent he received for houses in the Independence School District. "Let our people go!" Wrabec implored Taylor. The remark generated gleeful howls from many in the audience, and would be oft-repeated by media covering the event.

Addressing the issue of a boundary change, Taylor plainly told the crowd, "We cannot afford to lose 2,200 students and [their] families who have been integral to our success." When a woman asked Taylor if the change would reprise desegregation issues, he replied ominously, "No one would want to revisit any of those issues that were tried in that case. It would cost an enormous amount of money and time." The remark provoked murmuring across the theatre.

Hinson's answers to questions were usually briefer than Taylor's elaborate responses. The first question Hinson received came from a woman wondering about implications of potential boundary change: "What happens to the children if this goes through?" Hinson replied simply that Western Independence schools "would remain open, viable neighborhood schools," a remark that generated instant applause.

To other inquiries, Hinson asserted that the Independence School District would remain annexation-neutral unless a ballot would allow affected citizens to vote in the matter and, in addition, it became certain that annexation would not financially burden the school district. "The Independence School District has taken a position of neutrality in this issue," he said. "The goal of the administration and board of the Independence School District is to gather information in regard to the many questions that we have that remain unanswered, in addition to understanding people's concerns," he said.

The Independence School District was working to determine what financial requirement might be needed to re-fit and re-inventory the seven Kansas City School District schools if they were annexed, Hinson allowed. "Neighborhood schools are our priority," said Hinson, again generating thunderous applause.

Throughout the forum, Callahan spoke emotionally about democracy in "Harry S. Truman's home town." He had introduced legislation—

Missouri Senate Bill 602—to start a process for achieving boundary change. Such an initiative would require a petition and voting process.

"I'd like to thank Senator Callahan for fighting this fight for us— please don't give up!" begged a woman given the microphone as the two-hour forum drew to a close. Her remark almost brought down the house with applause. Callahan beamed; Hinson grinned. Taylor looked down at the table.

Headlines in the next day's *The Examiner* regional newspaper proclaimed "Packed House at School Forum...Most Say Change is Needed." A barrage of stories and letters to the editor about school boundary change issues soon started appearing in local media as the community embraced the issue, began to analyze it, praise it, question it and wonder if annexation would ever happen.

Two more public forums on the issue, with the same featured speakers, were scheduled by Progress Independence for coming weeks. But Taylor did not show up for either of them. By July, he had left the Kansas City School District, working as Superintendent of schools in Grand Rapids, Michigan.

Taylor's five-year tenure as superintendent in Kansas City was among the district's longest in more than 30 years. Anthony Amato, Superintendent of public schools in New Orleans, Louisiana, whom Hinson had never met and did not know, was appointed to replace Taylor.

———————

Blake Roberson
President, Board of Education

Blake Roberson is a graduate of Truman High School in the Independence School District. His family has lived in the Independence area for generations. Today, he operates a successful State Farm Insurance agency. He was elected President of the Independence School District Board of Education in April 2008, after serving as a board member since 2000.

"The Independence School District Board of Education and Superintendent Dr. Jim Hinson enthusiastically endorsed annexation of seven schools from the Kansas City School District immediately after the November 6, 2007, election when voters in both districts voted overwhelmingly in favor of school boundary change," he says.

"The annexation movement became a kind of 'perfect storm' across our community after State Senator Victor Callahan was able to change the school boundary law and the annexation issue appeared on the ballot. Our Board of Education felt we had a moral and ethical obligation to investigate the positive aspects of annexation, which we did thoroughly starting more than a full year before the annexation vote occurred.

"We believed we had an opportunity and a responsibility to help change our community by using education to boost a positive outlook for students and their families and help rebuild neighborhood pride. Our community, along with teachers, staff and administrators at the Independence School District, united in this commitment.

"Thousands of citizens in Western Independence and Sugar Creek have put their faith in the Independence School District to provide new educational opportunities for their children after enduring years of disappointment with the Kansas City School District," he says.

"The outcome for patrons of the Independence School District has been very positive. I believe this story needs to be told and shared with other school districts across the nation."

2

Confronting the Issues

"The Kansas City School District just had a bad reputation."

Rick Hemmingsen, CEO, Independence Chamber of Commerce

In May 2000, *The New York Times* published a story under the headline "'F' for Kansas City Schools Adds to the District's Woes." The district's failures help explain the grassroots rebellion that residents of Western Independence and Sugar Creek undertook to improve the destiny of their schools, and why most local residents so desperately wanted change.

Public schools in Western Independence and Sugar Creek had been controlled by the Kansas City School District since 1955. In 1977, the Kansas City Board of Education filed a lawsuit against the state of Missouri and several federal agencies, alleging that their laws and regulations caused racial segregation in the Kansas City School District. When the case reached court seven years later, Federal District Judge Russell G. Clark realigned the Kansas City School District and named it a defendant in the action, rather than a plaintiff.

In 1986 Judge Clark found the state of Missouri and the Kansas City School District jointly liable for contributing to segregation in the district; he ordered both to spend what amounted to nearly $2 billion to desegregate the district. Most of the money, about $1.5 billion, was paid by the state.

Yet many authorities believed the outcomes were abysmal. In his article "Lessons from the Kansas City Desegregation Experiment" published by The Cato Institute, education writer Paul Ciotti wrote, "Test scores did not rise; the black-white gap did not diminish; and there was less, not greater, integration."

In 1995, the U.S. Supreme Court faulted Judge Clark's rulings, leading to a decision to end desegregation funding starting in 1999. In 1996, a *Time* magazine article stated "When the history of court-ordered school desegregation is written, Kansas City may go down as its Waterloo." Anyone who questioned such criticism needed only to look at the Kansas City School District's administrative revolving door: Between 1989 and 1997, the district had 10 different superintendents—an abnormal turnover for most school districts.

Charley Dumsky was Sugar Creek's mayor from 1993 until 1999. His children attended school in both the Kansas City and Independence School Districts. Dumsky believes the Kansas City School District "wanted to get better educated students, both black and white, but for some reason the board members could not get along and, when the board couldn't get along, nothing really good transpired. They would start some kind of a program; it would last a couple of years, stop, and [the board would] start something else."

Many local citizens believed the district's problems were one of the major drags on the western side of Independence and Sugar Creek.

That was nothing new. Independence voters tried to annex those schools in 1974 but Kansas City voters defeated them. The district's poor performance and concerns about crime deterred people from living in nearby neighborhoods.

Rick Hemmingsen viewed the situation as chief executive of the Independence Chamber of Commerce. Homes on streets served by the Kansas City School District "were not selling. Their market value was 20 percent lower than identical houses across the street in the Independence School District. The Kansas City School District," he says, "just had a bad rep."

Steve Mauer, an attorney with the Bryan Cave law firm in Kansas City and member of the Independence Chamber of Commerce, observes, "Whether you looked at it from a business perspective, a real estate perspective, from an education perspective, everything kept pointing to the Kansas City School District—that was the problem. Until you tackled that one thing, nothing else could get fixed. It became painfully obvious that something had to be done about the Kansas City School District, and that was not a new revelation."

Jim Hinson was chosen to lead the Independence School District in 2002 after being hired in 2001 as deputy superintendent for business and finance. He assumed the job as the district was entering the most challenging period in its history, fueled by Kansas City School District issues, state budget cuts for public education and, in 2002, launch of a "Comprehensive School Improvement Plan."

Under Hinson's direction and that of the seven-member Board of Education, this plan would renew the district's vision, mission and values. It would "improve quality of life through education;" work to ensure that "every student gains skills and self-confidence to be successful;" and provide more than 11,000 K-12 students with "safe, orderly and caring environments."

These photos show some of the poor physical conditions that appalled taxpayers in Independence and Sugar Creek whose children attended schools in the Kansas City School District. In some schools, steam pipes and sewer pipes leaked, and toilets wouldn't flush. Walls, partitions and lockers were damaged; floors and carpets were filthy. Fire code violations abounded. Citizens wanted positive change.

Hinson grew up in Carthage, a community of 11,000 in Missouri's southwest corner. His father, a minister, and his mother, a sixth-grade teacher, had taught him that "education can be a ticket for a better way of life." As a youth he was a fisherman, a hunter, a sports fan and reader of many books; one of his favorites was the classic "Where the

Red Fern Grows" about a boy and his two dogs whose loyalty influenced the young man's future outlook.

In a grocery store, Hinson worked his way through Missouri Southern University to earn a bachelor's degree; then earned master's and educational specialist degrees from Southwest Missouri State University. Before coming to Independence, he was a teacher and a principal in Carthage schools; he served as superintendent in two small Missouri school districts, and earned his Ed.D. from Saint Louis University.

Announcing Hinson's appointment in 2002, Board President Paul Roberts, Jr. said Hinson was unequivocally the right man for the job. The new superintendent, then 39, had distinguished himself with astute management of district finances and resources; he possessed natural leadership skills; his vision was to address the needs of "the whole student;" and he was a capable advocate of district policies, procedures and goals.

"My first priority is communication—getting to know more people on a deeper level and enhancing our levels of collaboration [with community partners]," Hinson told *The Examiner* newspaper.

From the start, people approached him to ask if his district could "take over" Kansas City School District schools in Western Independence and Sugar Creek. "A lot of people talked about it constantly to me," he says. But Hinson always remained neutral, replying that a great deal more would need to be learned about any such potential undertaking.

He set to work on the "Comprehensive School Improvement Plan" to increase student achievement; align programs and services for continuity; and maximize resources to better facilitate learning. Also, he had a school district with an annual budget of more than $110 million to run.

Across Independence, people saw what the Board of Education knew when Hinson assumed the superintendent's job—here was a tough, smart administrator, a leader who put the best interests of schools and students at the top of his priorities. He was scrupulously honest, fair-minded. He could motivate people. Importantly, in the words of the local political establishment, he could "take the heat."

Further, he was passionate about his work, clocking 60-hour weeks in the office and, in the evenings, making presentations to PTA groups, neighborhood meetings and civic committees. "He had me at 'Hello'" jokes Lois McDonald, a community volunteer and mother of 12 children whose youngest attended Procter Elementary School where Hinson hosted a session.

"He was honest about the issues faced in the schools; he acknowledged that they would be addressed; and he followed through on addressing them," McDonald says. "I knew he was a man of integrity, a man of his word. As a community volunteer, I would do whatever was asked of me by someone like that."

―――――――――

Media exposure of the first Englewood Theatre forum framed Hinson in the public eye as a cautious man in the middle of a very controversial issue. From then on, reporters dogged him. He became a sounding board for commentary about high quality public education.

Reflecting on that forum and the potential for school boundary change, Hinson admits, "The intensity of our conversation about our district's willingness to look at school boundary change only increased." That remark typifies his low-key style as a school superintendent noted for understatement rather than exaggeration. In his heart, Hinson, the father of three grown children, was as enthusiastic about potential school boundary change as anyone at the first forum. As a responsible public official, he just didn't show it, at least not then.

More than a year later, at another forum hosted by Progress Independence just weeks before the school boundary change issue appeared on Independence and Kansas City election ballots, Hinson responded to a question that could have been asked at the February 2006 forum.

It concerned the influence of families and neighborhood schools on student achievement and community cohesiveness.

Passionately, in a straightforward fashion and without notes, Hinson responded and, in so doing, showed the audience where his heart and hopes lay: "Families and neighborhoods are extremely important in the success of students at schools, along with everything else a school can do to endeavor to work with students and those families," he began. "Let me visit briefly with you about neighborhood schools because we throw this concept around frequently, 'we' being the Independence School District...

"A neighborhood school is a location that is in close proximity to the students, families and residents. In many cases, it's close enough so that some can walk to their neighborhood elementary school. There are activities at the school that encourage parents and families of those students, but also neighbors of those schools who may no longer have children at the school, to be actively engaged with that school where, hopefully, neighborhood activities occur as well. Families are engaged not only with their child but maybe also in adult education or other resources that family might need—that's going to occur at the neighborhood school."

"At the middle school and high school levels, obviously, you are going to have 'feeder' elementary schools for those locations. Those feeder schools are locations where the neighborhood school concept has been built (a model endorsed by the national Coalition for Community Schools). You have strong Parent Teacher Associations. You have strong Caring Community Site Councils—and they do work hand-in-hand with each other. [Caring Community Councils provide a range of student and family services supported by the not-for-profit Local Investment Commission at locations across the Independence School District.]

"Families and parents understand that schools are *more* than places where their child receives an education; they are also places where parents and families can receive services and assistance and resources that they need. That's a very important part of this process.

"But when you look at Nowlin Middle School and Van Horn High School [both then managed by the Kansas City School District]..." Here Hinson paused then said, "Van Horn cannot be, it is *impossible* for Van Horn to be, a neighborhood school with the current set up.

"How can you bus students from the city of Kansas City for an hour or longer...How can you bus those students away from their families for that period of time to Van Horn and then expect their families to be actively engaged in that school? That just doesn't happen...No, that doesn't work for neighborhood schools and it doesn't work for families.

"Ladies and gentlemen, let's understand this concept....That's not how you engage families. Neighborhood schools, hopefully, are designed to address the needs of the *entire family* and the neighbors of those schools."

Seeing Hinson acknowledge the school boundary issues at the forums filled people with anticipation. Excitement about potential annexation infested Western Independence; optimism swelled, especially among parents whose children attended schools there.

The Independence School District Board of Education was moved by the display. "We didn't understand the frustration, anger and passion for it until people got up one after another at the forum, begging us to do something to make it happen. There was a groundswell of hope," asserts Board Member Susan Jones.

Jana Waits, another Board member who attended, says, "It was the first public gathering of its kind for everyone to see and, after you saw it, the issue kept building on itself." Eileen Weir notes, "It gave everybody in a position of power in the city an undeniable message that this is what people wanted."

Soon after the event a *Kansas City Star* columnist wrote that if students in the Kansas City School District were annexed they "would benefit from Independence's higher-caliber school system." Fervent letters published in *The Examiner* in weeks that followed encouraged Hinson and the Independence School District to move forward with annexation.

Western Independence and Sugar Creek became a staging ground for an uprising that inspired residents to organize in churches, living rooms and door-knocking campaigns displaying dedication and passion for achieving their goal.

But the night that Hinson had offered his perspectives about neighborhood schools, his own future was in doubt. A few months earlier he was hospitalized for the first time in his life—twice—with a severe malady that baffled medical specialists for weeks on end. They told him he might have a brain tumor, multiple sclerosis, a viral infection or lyme disease.

When hospitalized, Hinson, accustomed to working 80-hour weeks, had his administrative assistant Annette Miller bring correspondence, memos and other papers to him daily so he could work from his hospital room. In October 2007, he spent four days at the Mayo Clinic in Rochester, Minn., undergoing more tests.

While the illness slowed him down for a time, it did not divert Hinson from his mission to represent and pursue the best interests of the Independence School District, its students, parents, and the community, as well as those of his Board of Education. Especially after all the challenges that he, the school district, Western Independence and Sugar Creek residents had dealt with over the previous 18 months and would encounter continuously as the drive to annex Kansas City schools accelerated.

More months would pass before he learned the potential cause of his medical condition. During that time, Hinson experienced more personal and professional challenges than ever before as he led the Independence School District in its public fight.

———

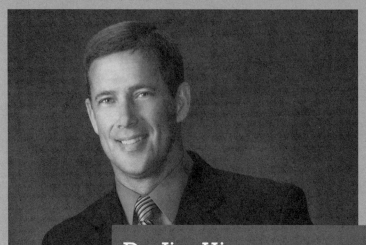

Dr. Jim Hinson
Superintendent, Independence School District

Jim Hinson's leadership as Superintendent of the Independence School District in the most emotionally-charged period in its history inspired people in all walks of life to realize their goal of changing their children's educational future and their community for the better.

Many people in Western Independence and neighboring Sugar Creek saw their children's educational prospects as dim until Hinson came forward in 2007 favoring annexing seven schools in their neighborhoods from the Kansas City School District.

A soft-spoken administrator who grew up in rural Carthage, Missouri, and worked his way through college, Hinson favors the concept of neighborhood schools serving "the whole student." He believes that public school districts should assume civic leadership roles by supporting partnerships between people and organizations that can help make their communities stronger.

Hinson helped unite community leaders and thousands of citizens who believed their children deserved greater educational opportunities. Those citizens successfully annexed the schools by voting overwhelmingly for district boundary change. What followed was a celebration called the Extreme School Makeover that united the community.

Residents in Western Independence and Sugar Creek now benefit from newly motivated teachers and a broader range of educational and extracurricular programs in the annexed schools. Parents and students have a positive new outlook. Families with young children are moving to the neighborhoods. New businesses are opening.

For his part in the initiative, accomplished after two years of legislative changes, petitions, lawsuits, arbitration hearings and delays, Hinson asserts he played a small role. "We believed that to resolve some of the educational and social ills of our community, our effort had to address the 'entire picture' and that everybody—city and economic development entities, churches, neighborhood groups and our school district—had to pull together. That's what happened here.

"Passion for the initiative and hope for the future expressed by so many people is very evident and continues to inspire us."

Written by Jeff Dunlap

3

The Politician

Tall, outspoken and ambitious, Independence native and Missouri State Senator Victor E. Callahan got his name by being born on July 4, 1963. His parents called him Victor E.

"I am a product of the Independence School District," he likes to say. People knowing him well assert that Callahan is an astute political thinker, an idealist, and something of a romantic packed into a driven, high-energy personality. In conversations, he often quotes William Shakespeare, philosophers, presidents and humanitarians to amplify or support his points of view.

These traits fueled Callahan's mission, starting in 2004, to find a way to resolve the distressing situation confronting Western Independence and Sugar Creek. For Callahan, freeing the communities' schools from Kansas City School District control became a crusade.

Some people thought he was a dubious candidate for the task because his experience in state politics was minimal, and that he would never pull it off. The idea seemed insurmountably complicated, fraught with legal challenges and potentially cost-prohibitive for the Independence School District. But his Irish blood and quixotic nature, and the fact that he felt he was in the right place at the right time, may have spurred his impulse.

All his life, Callahan has lived within five blocks of the Independence Square in the shadow of the Jackson County Courthouse and its statue of Harry S. Truman. His father was a lawyer who worked at the Lake City Ammunition Plant on the northeast end of town; his mother was a homemaker. At the dinner table, Joe Callahan made young Victor recite the names of all the U.S. presidents in order and nurtured his interest in history.

Callahan, a graduate of William Chrisman High School in north Independence, has been involved in politics for most of his life. At age 24, in 1988, two years after graduating from the University of Missouri-Kansas City, Callahan ran for the Independence City Council 2nd District seat—and he won. Many locals remember Councilman Callahan as a "young Turk," often brash, a "scrapper" with the capacity to sometimes rub people the wrong way. They also describe him as "scary smart." "He never forgets anything that he knows about anybody," says civic activist Donna Pittman, long-time owner of Curt's Famous Meats, a deli and butcher shop in Western Independence.

In 1994, Callahan was elected to the Jackson County legislature, where he continued to be outspoken. When State Senator Ron DePasco died in office in 2003, Callahan replaced him after winning a special election; the term was due to expire in November 2004. Callahan launched his re-election bid for 11th District Missouri State Senator on the platform of improving education in Western Independence and Sugar Creek.

"I had many critics," he recalls, speaking in a two-room office on East Walnut Street in Independence where he conducts official business locally. It sits about 120 miles from the state capitol in Jefferson City—where in political season Callahan can be found at least three days a week—and 100 feet from a tiny house where he lived with his parents when growing up.

"People thought what I said about improving the schools in Western Independence was for political reasons and that my position was just a ploy," says Callahan. "Or they thought nothing could be done to change the school situation."

He appealed to taxpayers by exhorting that the Kansas City School District was deficient in its service to students in Western Independence and Sugar Creek, a stigma to the neighborhoods' economy, and that remedies should be investigated and applied as soon as possible.

"The people of Western Independence agreed with everything I was saying, but the commentary was, 'That'll never happen.' They thought I was doing it for a political manipulation." Before Callahan won the democratic primary in August 2004, and triumphed in the state senatorial election in November, he created The 11th Senatorial District Task Force for the Improvement of Education in Western Independence and Sugar Creek. Its members were influential local leaders in business, education and government who began to poll citizens on educational quality and school safety.[2]

In its first report, based on surveys and public hearings, the Task Force declared that 94.6 percent of 2,400 survey respondents wanted to exit the Kansas City School District. The Task Force recommended changing the state school boundary statute and pursuing all options for school change in Western Independence, including, potentially, charter schools or even an entirely new school district. The question was...how?

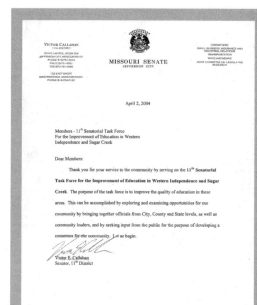

In 2004, Missouri State Senator Victor Callahan created the 11th Senatorial District Task Force for the Improvement of Education in Western Independence and Sugar Creek. Its members polled citizens on educational quality and school safety. In its first report, the Task Force declared that 94.6 percent of 2,400 survey respondents wanted to exit the Kansas City School District. The Task Force recommended changing the state school boundary statute.

Attorney Dennis Waits, a graduate of Van Horn High School, served on the Task Force. He says the Kansas City School District had created "hard feelings in the community... You begin to see people almost lose their sense of identity and their spirit... The Kansas City School District really dealt with this area a little bit like we were the spot on the tail of the dog. You didn't get to do any wagging, you just got wagged.

"Van Horn people," he says, "were most unhappy about being in the Kansas City School District. It just continued to worsen, and the longer you had the management in Kansas City, the longer they ignored doing things in the Van Horn area that they needed to do.

"People got more and more resentful. People, for a long time, wanted to remove themselves from the Kansas City School District. However, for a long time, it appeared as though you would probably only cause real legal problems by doing that because it would appear to be a racial thing when, really, it wasn't. It was simply a matter of people wanting to have neighborhood schools, not bus their kids all over, and to come back to the idea of 'Where you live is where you go to school.'" For decades, local politicians "had campaigned against the busing and campaigned on the idea of getting the Van Horn area out of the Kansas City School District. While they had wonderful intentions, none were in a position to go forward and actually get it done. Finally," Waits says, "Victor made the commitment to do this... and Victor is a tireless worker; he is an extremely bright guy."

Lois McDonald says, "The real initiative became revitalization of Western Independence; specifically, people were concerned about real estate values, economic development, quality of life and the Kansas City School District."

"Everybody wanted to get out of the Kansas City School District," says Paul Wrabec, noting that when Callahan released his Task Force results, "It wasn't a question of if people wanted it but 'When do we start?' We worried... 'Are we going to form our own school district? Can we get into the Independence School District? Or are we going to need to have charter schools?'"

There also were serious legal considerations; notably, whether the Kansas City School District would sue the Independence School District for trying to implement school boundary change, a change that would require Kansas City to give up its enrollment of students, its property—and tax revenue—in Western Independence and Sugar Creek. For Hinson and the Independence School District Board of Education those were extremely valid concerns.

———————

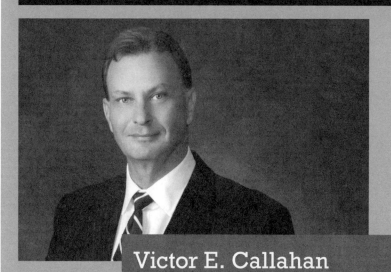

Victor E. Callahan
Missouri State Senator

In 2004, Missouri State Senator Victor E. Callahan began working to change laws that prohibited the Independence School District from annexing schools from the Kansas City School District. Previously, Callahan had served on the Jackson County legislature and Independence City Council.

"One reason I went into local government was that in 1987 my father had a massive stroke. He couldn't walk or feed himself. I moved into my parents' house to take care of him because it was too much for my mother to handle."

When Missouri State Senator Ron DePasco died in office in 2003, Callahan replaced him after winning a special election. On the morning of that election, Callahan's mother, Fay, died of a heart attack in his arms. From then on, Callahan, whose father died in 1996, put all his energies into politics.

Before elected to his first full term in 2004, Callahan formed a task force to study options for improving public education in Western Independence and Sugar Creek neighborhoods served by the Kansas City School District. He introduced legislation that, if passed, would set the stage for changing school boundary laws.

The Kansas City School District began an anti-annexation campaign in 2006. The senator's plan was cited as a "hostile takeover" effort that would, if successful, damage the district and potentially lead to legal actions.

Callahan persevered. In 2007, he introduced amendments to a bill that was later signed by Missouri Governor Matt Blunt enabling a boundary change vote. By a huge margin, the annexation ballot passed. Callahan became known as one of "The Four Horsemen" of Independence for his role in the annexation effort.

In September 2008, he was named "Independence Citizen of the Year" along with Dr. Jim Hinson, Steve Mauer and Pastor Bob Spradling for their history-making leadership roles in the turbulent initiative. That November, two days after he was again re-elected, Callahan was unanimously elected Democratic floor leader in the Missouri legislature.

4

Is This Feasible?

"We need to approach this with open minds."

Dr. Jim Hinson

One man knew how seriously Hinson felt about potential annexation: A burly, dark-eyed administrator who walked with a wide gait, Dr. Brian Mitchell. A native of Bolivar, Missouri, Mitchell had joined the Independence School District in 2005 as Associate Superintendent for Business and Finance—the role Hinson held before superintendent. From the start, Mitchell knew he would conduct due diligence to determine if annexing schools from the Kansas City School District would be financially feasible or a complete disaster.

"In my initial discussions with Dr. Hinson, before I even accepted the job," Mitchell recalls, "the question was 'What do you think about

Independence annexing Western Independence schools from the Kansas City School District?' My reply was, 'I think it would be great and I think it would happen if the voters had an opportunity to vote about it,'" Mitchell says.

Built like a football player, Mitchell talks with the patience of an elementary school teacher, which he was after earning two master's degrees from Southwest Baptist University and an Ed.D. at Saint Louis University. For five years before joining the district, Mitchell was Superintendent of schools in Fair Play, Missouri.

At the time of his arrival in Independence, "The poor performance of the Kansas City School District was well known," Mitchell says. "It was a conversation in the community for decades." He believed annexation would yield positive dividends for many reasons, one of which was that Western Independence, comprising 20 percent of the entire city, was economically distressed. Mitchell believed annexation would help "resuscitate" Western Independence. "I am a firm believer that communities are successful by and large because of educational services provided in the community," he says with passion. "When school districts offer successful programs and are excelling, you see a community thriving. When school districts are not successful, you see families with children move out. When that occurs, there is less stability for business owners.

"If you have kids and want them to have a quality education and opportunities to be successful in life, you've got to make a decision about where they are going to go to school." If a school district performs ineffectively, people "move out or send their kids to a private or parochial school," Mitchell says.

"As you see flight away from a community and lack of willingness of new residents to take their place, you start to see deterioration in that community. When you have less stability among families in a neighborhood, there is less stability for business owners to operate and have a clientele.

"As businesses choose to quit investing in that area they leave empty storefronts. Those empty storefronts deteriorate. Housing values decline...homes become rental properties...it perpetuates on itself. You have more of a transient population constantly moving in and out because there is less home ownership and less stability. Again, it cycles on itself."

Shortly before the first Englewood forum in 2006, Hinson gave the task of researching potential annexation to Mitchell. Hinson had notified the district's Board of Education that due diligence was underway but, initially, only Hinson and Mitchell knew the extent of those activities.

Mitchell describes his task, which would last more than two years, as enormously satisfying but, also, a "gut-wrenching experience." His research included forecasting potential needs for new staff and resources for educating 2,600 additional students entering the district if annexation, in fact, occurred. Also, Mitchell had to determine whether—in terms of assessed real estate values, potential tax revenue and funding from government sources—annexation would pay for itself.

"I went about it from the standpoint of what an annexation would really cost us, what it might generate in actual revenues without benefit of any additional money from other sources and *'Can we make this work?'*" His thinking was, *"If it is going to happen, it is going to have to work on its own merit."* (About forty-five percent of the district operating budget is funded by local tax revenue, 45 percent by the state of Missouri, and 10 percent federally funded.)

"With this approach, we had to make an important decision: Do we believe an annexation is in the best interests of our school district, our community and our people? My decision was absolutely 'yes.'"

Mitchell's office produced "formulas on top of formulas.... We developed many different scenarios based on what we knew and what we could find out." He had to consider teacher salaries, insurance benefits, books, supplies, technology needs, furnishings, maintenance and upkeep among other potential expenses. He kept his findings locked in a filing cabinet in his office.

One issue of major concern was whether the Missouri state funding formulas applied to the Independence School District might change if annexation occurred. Missouri school districts with substantial real estate assessed valuations and related tax income generally contribute more to their operating budgets than districts with lower real estate assessments; they also receive less state financial support.

Mitchell worried that some state authorities might consider a potential post-annexation increase of about $200 million in assessed real estate valuations for the Independence School District without fully considering the fiscal requirements of educating an additional 2,600 students. He would not learn the answer to that troubling question until June 2008.

As he worked through the research, Mitchell recalls, "It was hard to put aside emotions. No matter how much we wanted it to happen, an annexation had to make financial sense; it couldn't be something detrimental to kids and people in our school district.

"It would have been easy to put on blinders and say 'Let's do it!' and whatever the consequences may have been, deal with them after the fact. Sure, you have to have passion and commitment, but you must go through the due diligence of objectively evaluating 'Can this work?'... Be prepared to say 'no' if it won't," he adds.

By design, Hinson publicly said nothing more about the boundary issue in the months after the first Englewood forum except that the district would study its feasibility. To the Board of Education, his approach was conscientious and open. In December 2005, two months before the forum, Hinson advised board members that he was considering the district's future in the context of Callahan's Senate Bill 602.

The Independence School District Board of Education believed it had a moral and ethical obligation to investigate the potential impact of annexation, which it did thoroughly starting in 2006, more than a year before the annexation vote occurred. Those board members were, clockwise from top left: Ira Anders, Blake Roberson, Ken Johnston, Dr. Robert Clothier, Jana Waits, Susan Jones and Ann Franklin.

He told an inquiring reporter from *The Examiner*, Sarah Swedberg, that he intended to research the bill and its potential implications. "It is a very complex issue, and we're gathering as much information as we can," Hinson told Swedberg. "We need to approach this with open minds and find out what people think."

Hinson and the board routinely met twice a month to conduct district business. He thought, rightly so, that its seven members were concerned about Callahan's activities and the public's annexation fever. "All of the board members had basically lived in the community their entire lives ..." Hinson says. "I wasn't sure where they stood on the issue and I believed that they would be very apprehensive and very cautious. Of which they were."

Throughout most of 2006 he told the board, "I'm still not convinced absolutely that we need to do this, but we need to thoroughly investigate it." Hinson adds, "The board was very gracious to allow the administrative staff to gather information and to share that information with the [board members], which we did on a regular basis."

Many Independence officials, before Hinson's arrival a few years earlier, had warned the board that school boundary change "could never happen" and "could never work," says Hinson, noting, "They had observed what had taken place through the desegregation process and court hearings in that regard." Yet public pressure on the board increased.

Ira Anders, a retired elementary school teacher elected to the board in 2004, recalls that in 2006, "We had people come to school board meetings to ask us to get involved in the issue, and to ask whether or not we supported it, and people asked me if I supported it. But at that time we didn't know all the ramifications and we didn't know about the debt that might come or the buildings [that the Kansas City School District managed] or anything.

"My analogy was that it would be like you were coming to the school board to ask us to adopt a science textbook when the only thing we've seen is the cover of the book. We don't know what's inside," Anders says.

As fervor for annexation spread across the community, Hinson says, some board members grew apprehensive. "'What would the cost entail for the school district?' 'Would this violate a desegregation court order?' 'Would it reignite the entire desegregation process?'" members wondered. "Certainly there was a right for concern," Hinson says.

"The board members wanted to make sure they protected the Independence School District as it existed, prior to any annexation. They were willing, certainly, to bring on schools in Western Independence and Sugar Creek but they were very cautious that it could be devastating to the Independence School District.

"Yet," Hinson adds, "I don't think the board ever doubted that, if we could get through the legal process and the financial process, that it would be successful."

Though noncommittal about annexation, Hinson began discussing the issue with teachers and administrative staff. He met in groups with virtually every teacher and staff member to gain their opinions. "Employees of the Independence School District knew they could turn around the educational environment for kids in Western Independence and Sugar Creek if we could get through the legal and financial hurdles," he says.

Ann Franklin, a district board member, reflected on annexation fervor: "We felt it was our responsibility to know and to provide information to Independence School District voters...The implication was that we would prepare to do this [annexation] if the voters approved it."

Through the cold winter of 2006, Hinson and Mitchell escalated their research, gathering "as much information as we could possibly gather relating to desegregation, relating to any previous annexation issues in the state of Missouri, looking at any precedents that might exist," Hinson says. In considering annexation, "I wanted to make sure the board made very educated, very thoughtful decisions—not decisions made upon threats, allegations, fears or emotions."

It was indeed a season of change. With letters to media, many citizens fueled annexation fever. Candidates for local elections upcoming in April waved the banner of annexation with guarded enthusiasm.

Bill Lockhart's letter published in *The Examiner* stated "Those of us who have children and live in Western Independence want, no, we *demand* to send our kids to the Independence School District so they can get a great education." Lucy Young, an incumbent city council candidate, told a reporter, "We must hold the Kansas City School District accountable for the education of our children ... if we do not change the education process, our city's western and northern areas will continue to be affected. Property values will continue to decline and young families with children will continue to consider other areas to live in ...".

Bob Buckley, Sugar Creek city attorney, wrote *The Examiner*, asking, "Can anyone in the Kansas City School District seriously contend that the students in Western Independence and Sugar Creek will not receive a better education in the Independence School District under the leadership of Superintendent Jim Hinson and our current school board?"

He explained legal procedures for a school boundary vote to occur as they then existed under state statutes. "If Callahan's bill becomes law," Buckley wrote, "there would undoubtedly be a legal challenge to it. I can't predict the future, but I suspect we will be talking about this subject for several years as it moves from public forums to legislation to the courts."

But Senate Bill 602 would not become Missouri law. By late 2006 Callahan was changing its language so he could reintroduce it in the senate. The senator also favored a "backup plan" for creating charter schools in case strategies for enabling an annexation vote failed.

"Victor had a political chess game going on multiple chess boards," observes Stacie Short, who knew Callahan well and promoted economic growth in Western Independence with her husband Monte, a two-time president of the Englewood Business Association.

That summer, Hinson met the new Superintendent of the Kansas City School District, Anthony Amato, for the first time. Amato had replaced Dr. Bernard Taylor that July. They met in Amato's office. "It was a very friendly, cordial meeting," recalls Hinson, who made a diplomatic outreach to Amato to welcome him to his new job.

As their conversation ensued, Hinson says he told Amato, "'There is an issue between our two school districts about annexation, an issue you need to know about.'

"He said, 'I'm not aware of it. Nobody has brought this to my attention,'" recalls Hinson, who then suggested to Amato, "'Well, I'm sure your PR department has the video of that forum. Why don't you take a look at that video and give me a call.'"

Hinson's intent was not to press Amato at all, he says, merely to inform him of the school district scenario peer-to-peer. But Amato never called Hinson back.

The next time the two superintendents met was months later, in December. The meeting would involve more than just the two men, and its outcome was not a happy one. It became a declaration of war.

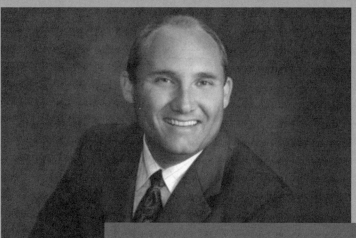

Dr. Brian Mitchell
Right-Hand Man

Dr. Brian Mitchell was hired as Associate Superintendent for Business and Finance for the Independence School
District in 2005 knowing his responsibility, among others,
was to conduct due diligence to determine if annexing
seven schools from the Kansas City School District would
be feasible. A native of Bolivar, Missouri, he served as Dr.
Jim Hinson's "right-hand man" during the annexation in
addition to managing day-to-day district operations.

"The annexation favorably impacts thousands of people in Western Independence, and will impact generations of people in Independence for many years to come,"
Mitchell says. "The community is experiencing a rebirth
of positive attitudes and new hope—I think annexation is
the most important thing to have happened in Independence since Harry S. Truman was elected President.

"Improvement of instructional programs is taking place
in every classroom, and is already exponentially better in
those schools. There is a genuine effort by city leaders to

take advantage of the annexation. Motivation and momentum for economic development are growing."

Mitchell played a key role preparing for arbitration hearings to settle financial disputes between the two school districts. His tactical planning for the Extreme School Makeover of July 2008 was crucial. After that event, Mitchell was asked by the Board of Education in Jefferson City, Missouri, to be its superintendent. Making his decision was difficult since he and his family deeply loved Independence. Ultimately, Mitchell could not turn down the job of leading the district in Missouri's state capitol. He started there July 1, 2009.

"I told the Board of Education in Jefferson City that I expect we would do great, great things. Being honest, I also said that the Independence School District annexation process, no matter what I may accomplish in the rest of my career, was truly the most rewarding year-and-a half that I will ever experience professionally."

5

The Gauntlet

"They are going to fight to the last level of absurdity."

Victor Callahan, Missouri State Senator

Fat flakes of wet snow blanketed the parking lot on Sunday, December 31, 2006, as Pastor Bob Spalding nosed his pickup truck into a space near the back door of Maywood Baptist Church on Winner Road a few blocks from the Englewood Theatre. Striding down the long corridor to his big, comfortable office in the lower level, he checked his BlackBerry for text messages before greeting his secretary Kathleen Wright. Like Spradling, she had arrived early to prepare for morning services and stood by the steps ascending to the church's stained-glassed sanctuary.

Spradling was especially busy, anticipating packed pews for his New Year's sermon and throngs of parishioners approaching the altar midway through the service to proclaim their faith in God and receive his blessings—prayerful words of encouragement issued, and a pat on their shoulders.

The pastor guarded many secrets shared by his congregation, but that day Spradling possessed one of his own. Recently he had been called to a confidential meeting at City Hall by Don Reimal, the new Mayor of Independence and longtime member of Maywood's congregation. The purpose was to explain a political strategy for annexing seven schools managed by the Kansas City School District to the men who would lead the initiative.

In the New Testament Book of Revelations, the "four horsemen of the apocalypse" are described in verse as metaphors of Famine, War, Conquest and Death. But Spradling attended that meeting as a horseman of a very different kind: a community leader drawn into a mission to instill new life in the neighborhoods where Maywood Baptist is a rock of faith and spiritual hope for hundreds of people.

Tall, broad-shouldered, handsomely bald and with a deep, booming voice, Spradling, a native of Cape Girardeau, Missouri, started ministering at age 19 while attending Southeast Missouri State University. He was a pastor in small churches in Mississippi, Louisiana and in Charleston, Missouri, before arriving in Independence. He is well-known in Independence, where the faith-based community has 156 churches, as a powerful, influential presence, tirelessly involved with charities and neighborhood improvement.

"If the tone of Pastor Bob's voice was a half-step lower, he would sound just like Johnny Cash," says a parishioner with a chuckle. "But the best thing you can say about Pastor Bob when he sings hymns is that it's loud," adding "everyone in the congregation adores him. He does *so much* for this community."

Spradling had been concerned about conditions in Western Independence for decades. "The day I came to town in 1984," he recalls, "I was given a tour of the city. The decline of this community was something to address from the very beginning, particularly from the church standpoint. In the 1970s, Maywood's attendance was in the 700s. When I came to Maywood, it was 254. Many people did not want to live in the neighborhood and anyone who could move out moved." More than a few members told him "We are moving so we can put our kids in another school district."

"I don't know if you can put all the blame for that on the Kansas City School District," Spradling says. "About that time there was an industrial decline" after several local manufacturing plants closed or downsized in the early 1980s. "Men had lost their jobs. The whole of Western Independence and Northeast Kansas City was negatively impacted. From the church standpoint, Maywood had lost about 50 members a year," recalls the pastor, noting that his own and other neighborhood churches struggled to replace members who moved away.

Yet soon after he arrived at Maywood, Spradling began to make a positive difference. Church members raised funds to renovate its auditorium, applying new paint, wall-to-wall carpeting, choir chairs, pew covers, drapes and lighting—and installed a new sound system with a big video screen behind the altar so psalms and Bible verses could be seen by all in the sanctuary.

Maywood began to expand its neighborhood outreach programs, interfaith prayer groups and local ministries. Little by little, the congregation began to grow, doubling its membership. But economic and social conditions surrounding the church continued to decline as many homes became rental properties, businesses closed and complaints about the Kansas City School District, which had some 22 superintendents between 1978 and 2008, escalated.

When Spradling arrived in Mayor Reimal's office for the meeting, he found State Senator Victor Callahan, attorney Steve Mauer and, sitting quietly in a corner, Jim Hinson, who had admitted publicly nothing more but that he was studying the feasibility of school boundary change. Excitedly, Callahan proposed to introduce new legislation in the Missouri Senate that, if passed, would enable the annexation issue to appear on local ballots in 2007.

Mauer stood up—he was helping the senator prepare language for a new bill. Both men detailed mandatory steps the community had to take for the annexation ballot to occur, starting with getting the legislation passed in both houses of the Missouri General Assembly, having it signed into law by then-Governor Matt Blunt, and initiating a public petition to facilitate the ballot.

Callahan later admitted, "Dr. Hinson's opinion was, to me, the only relevant opinion in the room at that moment." That's because, as a political subdivision in Missouri, the Independence School District Board of Education and Hinson, by law, would need to endorse a school boundary change and announce intentions to pursue annexation, and then go forward with the initiative. The meeting quickly supercharged when Hinson, after hearing him out, told Callahan that if the senator could get the state's school boundary law changed, enabling a municipal vote for annexation, the Independence School District would go for it.

"When Jim Hinson came out and said, 'It's the right thing for the community, it's the best thing for the kids, we need to do this'... that changed *everything*," recalls Mauer, then soon to be 2007 board chairman of the Independence Chamber of Commerce. "Hinson was saying, 'I will make this happen if you can get it into my district...' Victor Callahan was saying 'I will change the law so ... you can get it on the ballot ...' Pastor Bob was there and he's got an impeccable reputation ... Pastor Bob says he'll 'Get it done ...' When I saw all that, I knew we had the components that we really needed."

Pastor Spradling recalls, "I was very impressed with Steve Mauer's preparation and presentation of the annexation plan. I expressed my willingness to contribute whatever I could to the process. It would be very much of a team effort, a very ambitious effort, and I remember saying to myself: 'OK, here we go!'"

Callahan, Spradling, Mauer and Hinson later would be nicknamed "The Four Horsemen of Independence" by volunteers they recruited to help manage the complicated initiative. Mayor Reimal pledged to assist as best he could as an elected official to promote the cause. The men agreed to total confidentiality until Callahan could, they hoped, achieve their goal in the Republican-dominated state legislature. All five men bowed their heads. Spradling closed the meeting with a prayer, hoping that the team would be successful.

Hinson's next task was to make another courtesy call to Anthony Amato, Superintendent of the Kansas City School District. He attended that meeting in Amato's office with Callahan, Mayor Reimal, Sugar Creek Mayor Stan Salva, State Representative Ray Salva whose 51st District served Sugar Creek, and Ira Anders from the Independence School District Board of Education. Beside Amato, on his side of the conference table, sat several Kansas City School District officials with notepads.

"The agenda was the annexation," says Hinson. "We had a very cordial meeting with Mr. Amato and the others and we said... 'This is an issue that we'd really like to see happen. We don't want to attack the Kansas City School District. We want to do this in a friendly fashion. Can we figure out some way to sit down and work on this or at least look at it from a collective perspective?' "Their response," says Hinson, "was 'We'll talk about it with our Governmental Relations Subcommittee of the board and we will get back with you.'" The meeting ended.

Days passed. "They didn't get back with us," says Hinson. "So, finally, I called Mr. Amato to say, 'I haven't heard from you, what's going to happen?' He said, 'We're going to oppose it.'"

"You know," Hinson says, "I always try to be fair in any type of disagreement; I have a tendency to put my cards on the table. If you want to fight about something, we're going to fight about it. But, I'm not going to do it behind your back. The intent, at that time, was to not embarrass the Kansas City School District, not attack them publicly... to keep everything above board, to sit down and see if we could work out this issue together." Unfortunately, Hinson says, "They weren't interested in that occurring."

Amato and the Kansas City School District Board of Education may have thrown down the gauntlet, but Amato would not be around for all of the fight. He was the district's 24th Superintendent since 1969. After 18 months on the job, Amato resigned in January 2008 after a dispute with the board. Yet he would remain in the job long enough to witness the display of determination, energy and faith that Independence and Sugar Creek residents summoned in 2007 to change the destinies of their school district, their children and their community.

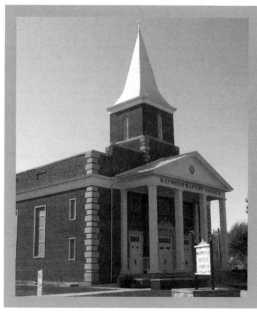

Maywood Baptist Church in Western Independence became a center for pro-annexation volunteer activities that spread across the community. Pastor Bob Spradling hosted inter-faith prayer meetings with ministers from other churches to pray for the annexation initiative. Hundreds of Maywood members, as well as volunteers not affiliated with the church, gathered to launch a pro-annexation petition drive in July 2007.

In fact, the Kansas City School District threw down the gauntlet long before Hinson's group met with Amato in December 2006. Calling it a "flare" to show his intentions to the Missouri General Assembly, Callahan had drafted Senate Bill 602 to lay a legal platform for school boundary change late in 2005. When he did, fireworks exploded in Kansas City.

In January 2006, just days before the first Englewood Theatre forum, the Kansas City School District launched an aggressive anti-annexation communications campaign. It mailed letters to parents and guardians of kids in Western Independence and Sugar Creek. The senator's plan was called a "hostile takeover" effort that, if successful, would result in 40 percent of the white students then attending Kansas City School District schools being transferred from the district, possibly leading to legal actions and potential reassertion of federal desegregation mandates.

"Legislation has been introduced in the Missouri Legislature that is designed to seize part of the territory of the Kansas City, Missouri, School District (KCMSD) that lies within the municipal boundaries of the cities of Independence and Sugar Creek and transfer that territory to the Independence School District," the letter began. "After reviewing the facts carefully," it declared, "... the board and administration of the Kansas City School District has decided to oppose this initiative in the strongest possible terms." If the legislation passed, the Kansas City School District "... would suffer a loss of revenue as a result of the transfer of thousands of students out of the district, which would then prompt the federal courts to consider another tax increase ..."

"This initiative stigmatizes the seven schools in the area where annexation is sought ... We flatly reject any suggestion that association with the KCMSD somehow diminishes the quality of life or the value of property in our neighborhoods," it said. The letter cited potential unknowns, including how much the Independence School District "would have to pay KCMSD for those properties ..." It closed with the guarantee, "Resolving this issue will be costly, distracting and divisive. Nevertheless, you can be confident in our resolve to successfully oppose this initiative."

The letter made no mention of the Kansas City School District's high dropout rate at Van Horn High in Western Independence, or that the district itself was only provisionally accredited since being disaccredited by the Missouri Department of Elementary and Secondary Education in 1999 for not achieving performance standards.

Some people who received the letter called it a "scare tactic." Others took it quite seriously. Callahan says, "I always had the belief that KC would fight us every step of the way. There were some people who thought, well, they'll give up. I said no, they will never give up. They are going to fight to the last level of absurdity."

———————

Pastor Bob Spradling
Powerful Presence

Pastor Bob Spradling is a powerful presence at Maywood Baptist Church in the working-class neighborhoods of Western Independence where he has ministered since 1984. In the arduous annexation initiative that some people liken to the Old Testament saga of David and Goliath, he was a guiding light, a source of spiritual encouragement and faith.

"It was very important for us in the faith community to do the most culturally relevant things we could do to involve ourselves with the annexation process," he says. "Many churches and people came on board; many worked extremely hard. We listened to people's concerns. We prayed for Independence. We prayed for Kansas City. We continue to be very involved today."

A native of Cape Girardeau, Missouri, Pastor Spradling became a devoted Baptist "when the Lord got a hold of me" between his high school senior year and freshman year at Southeast Missouri State University. At 19, while studying marketing at college, he began ministering at a country church in Perkins, Missouri, population 142.

Maywood Baptist became an operations center for the annexation drive that began in the summer of 2007. Pastor Spradling organized prayer meetings with ministers from nine other churches who gathered to support the initiative. He hosted an assembly at Maywood in July 2007 attended by 500 people, launching the petition drive that enabled the annexation vote to appear on local ballots. Yard signs built in Maywood's basement were distributed by scores of parishioners.

After the petition drive, church members made thousands of phone calls to promote the vote and turned out by the hundreds to participate in the Extreme School Makeover after the Independence School District successfully assumed control of the annexed schools.

Beloved in his community, Pastor Spradling is also secretary of the NorthWest Communities Development Corporation, a director of the Fairmount/Carlisle 353 Tax Abatement Board and a member of the local Tax Increment Financing Commission, all working to help build a greater future for Western Independence.

6

Prayers, Politics & Petitions

"New Law Gives Hope in Western Independence"

Headline in *The Examiner* daily newspaper

A perfect storm began to form in Western Independence and Sugar Creek early in 2007, stirring apprehension and anticipation. Like no other the communities had ever seen, its power began to build slowly as annexation fervor escalated.

"The Four Horsemen of Independence" were in the saddle. In neighborhoods all around, people approached them with expressions of hope, words of encouragement and questions of concern. Spradling, Mauer, Hinson and Callahan had, in fact, not known each other very well until they united in commitments favoring annexation, all aware that they were entering risky new territory with uncertain outcomes for Western Independence and Sugar Creek—and for their careers.

No annexation of schools or school boundary change of the size and scope they envisioned had ever occurred in America, so far as they knew.[3] No adversary as dominant as the Kansas City School District had ever vowed so aggressively that it would fight such a move. But people in neighborhoods that the four men served were desperate for change. As Eileen Weir would remark, "It was as if people were saying, 'If annexation doesn't occur, we might as well roll up the streets and forget about it.'" Donna Pittman described the dispute facing the community as "like David versus Goliath."

Spradling, the preacher, began spiritual groundwork, even though The Four Horsemen's ultimate goals and plans still were secret. He organized the first of many interfaith prayer meetings that occurred over the next six months, with pastors and members of ten local churches. The first took place on February 9 at Mount Washington United Methodist Church, near a particularly distressed area of Western Independence on Arlington Avenue, where the Reverend Jim Coffer was pastor.

"We had clergy from two Catholic, one Assembly of God, three Baptist, three Methodist and one Community of Christ church in those prayer meetings. All of those churches would figure into the faith-based aspect of the annexation," Spradling says in his deep, authoritative voice. At that first interfaith prayer meeting, Spradling recalls, "We extended prayer for an array of community needs, and we prayed for the schools in our area."

Hinson, who attends church services at Englewood Assembly of God in Western Independence, says, "The impact of the faith-based community was crucial in the overall process. The involvement of the pastors, ministers, priests and their congregations was extremely beneficial from the outset. They acted as an instrumental component."

Between March and July, "important planning meetings took place at Mayor Reimal's office," says Spradling. "This was the time when

Steve Mauer and Victor Callahan crafted the plan that would bring into law the necessary changes to state statutes to allow the boundary change vote to take place." Mauer describes those meetings in the Mayor's office as dealing with "the big issue" of the Kansas City School District by finding ways to "tackle the big gorilla" of legislative change.

Hinson knew about those meetings and, early in 2007, he hosted related meetings in his office at district headquarters on North Pleasant Street, yet they were informational in nature only. "I was not involved with creating the language of the new senate bills that Senator Callahan began working on. I really tried to stay out of that process. Victor tried to keep me out of that process as much as possible, and I wanted to stay out as much as possible."

One reason why: "There was fear that individuals in the Kansas City School District would file suit to try to reignite the desegregation issue, take it to court and try to involve the Independence School District." The Four Horsemen knew if that happened the Independence School District might be dragged into court for years, stalling any annexation initiative and potentially bankrupting the district.

"I tried *not* to lead the effort for a long time—I tried to *listen*," Hinson continues. "I met with every faculty and staff member in every building in our district in groups, and with every PTA, civic club, church and neighborhood organization that wanted to talk. I tried to share what we knew, but I really tried to listen and gain feedback from our community regarding the issue."

In January 2007, Callahan introduced a new version of the "flare" senate bill submitted a year earlier, calling this revision of SB602 a "distraction." Mauer called it a "Trojan horse."

"Victor is a very deft politician," asserts Mauer. "By having everybody looking at this bill out there, we had an opportunity to find a host of other bills where, if we changed four or five sentences, we could tack on our changes…" In other words, create amendments to other legislation that the Missouri House and Senate might consider which,

In the spring 2007 Missouri legislative session, State Senator Victor Callahan inserted language into 13 bills to enable a vote for the process of the Independence School District annexation to occur. Kansas City lobbyists quashed Callahan's amendments in 11 of those bills, but two of them passed, allowing a boundary change vote to appear on local ballots if legal steps, including a successful, pro-ballot petition drive, took place. Callahan is shown with then-State Senator Chris Koster and State Senator Ron Mayer in 2007.

if passed, would enable procedures for an annexation ballot to appear later in 2007.

"I know that politics is ultimately arithmetic," Callahan says, referring to votes. Yet that didn't mean he could get laws changed merely by filing a bill or amending others. He was a Democrat in a Republican-dominated legislature. With 522 public school districts in Missouri, not all legislators knew about the annexation issue.

In addition, Callahan worried whether the Missouri Department of Elementary and Secondary Education would object to a proposed school boundary change which might generate lawsuits and arbitration. For these reasons, he wanted Missouri's then-Governor Matt Blunt on his side.

"Even though he was a Republican, I had gone to Governor Blunt and said, 'You're not from Independence, but you've got to realize that this is very important...'" the senator says. Governor Blunt expressed an enlightened opinion about the potential annexation, says Callahan: "He was supportive of it." That would be helpful to Callahan if the time ever came when the senator had to ask the Governor to, as Callahan puts it, "use the red phone" to encourage more support.

In April 2007, Callahan began inserting proposed amendments into 13 different bills to enable a vote for annexation to occur if a pro-vote petition drive was successful. These included an addition to an existing bill, called "Missouri First Steps," which supported health services for developmentally disabled children that few legislators were expected to oppose.

To ensure that amendment was included in both House and Senate versions of "Missouri First Steps," Callahan approached members of the house leadership for their endorsement and involvement. He got it.

Why insert amendments into so many bills? Mauer and Callahan fully expected that Kansas City School District lobbyists would try to quash SB602 before it reached the Senate floor.

The frenzied final two weeks of the spring 2007 legislative session, when legislators worked around the clock to modify bills and lobbyists tried to get bills and amendments embellished or killed, were opportune for Callahan's deal-making. The senator kept his activities quiet. Few people in Independence and Jefferson City knew what he was doing. But lobbyists for the Kansas City School District succeeded in quashing Callahan's amendments in 11 of the 13 bills the senator modified.

Yet two of those bills, SB112 and SB221, passed in May with Callahan's amendments intact. Those bills allowed for a boundary change vote to take place if specific legal steps occurred, including a successful, pro-ballot petition drive by citizens in both the Independence and Kansas City School Districts. Western Independence and Sugar Creek citizens had no lobbyist for the issue. Mauer says, "We didn't need a lobbyist—we had Senator Callahan."

On June 27, Governor Blunt signed a new law changing the process for moving school district boundaries; the new law also extended the

"Missouri First Steps" program for developmentally disabled toddlers, which would have expired if the legislature hadn't voted to support it. Headlines in *The Examiner* proclaimed "New Law Gives Hope in Western Independence."

On its opinion page, the newspaper declared, "This week has seen important progress toward moving western Independence [schools] into the Independence School District. In the General Assembly, the driving force behind the measure Blunt signed has been state Sen. Victor Callahan, D-Independence. He has patiently and diligently worked on this issue for years, often when it seemed like a fruitless task. His hard work could well pay off, and the proposed changes would be the single best thing for improved education and economic revival in that part of our community."

A June 28 Associated Press wire report stated, "The Independence School District met all 14 performance standards in its 2006 review" by the Missouri Department of Elementary and Secondary Education. "Kansas City schools met just three of those standards..." (The Independence School District won the prestigious "Distinction in Performance" accreditation from the State Department of Education in 2006, also earning the distinction in 2007, 2008 and 2009.) The bill also allowed a public vote to occur at an earlier election than provided for under the old law, the report noted. This would prove crucial for the annexation because The Four Horsemen were in a hurry.

Thrilled, elated and energized about the new law, jubilant citizens celebrated until late at the Courthouse Exchange on the Independence Square and at Ernie's Steak House in Sugar Creek. Yet they would need to work very fast to carry out a successful petition drive to get the annexation vote placed on local ballots for the November 6 election.

A weary Callahan was circumspect. He knew managing the petition process that summer would be complicated by deadlines and much more; in particular, legal requirements to get thousands of signatures on both sides of the existing school boundary—from residents throughout the Independence School District and, also, in the Kansas City School District.

At the start of any petition, he knew, "People sit in a room and they go, 'Oh...We can get all the signatures.' But I go, 'Really? Have you done a petition drive before? It's not fun. It's walking in 100-degree heat, you work all day and you get 20 signatures when you need thousands.'" But that didn't worry Western Independence citizens priming for the task.

Always energetic and up for a challenge, Mauer was ready to create formal petition forms for different municipal neighborhoods to ensure their legal compliance, and to explain publicly how signatures legally could be acquired and be validated. Mauer didn't even live in Independence—but in Overland Park, Kansas. He had already donated many hours to help change the boundary law, but his *pro bono* commitment to annexation was just beginning. Although Mauer didn't know it, a battery of lawsuits and legal actions with the Kansas City School District were awaiting him and the Independence School District.

For Hinson, life was about to radically change, and not because of the petition drive or lawsuits on the horizon. That spring and summer, "I had dizziness, fatigue, lots of respiratory distress, muscle aches..." he says. "I had periods when I couldn't breathe, couldn't get a breath ...."

"I am used to working 80 hours a week and never blinking an eye. I try to stay fit and eat right. At first I just thought that I was tired from burning the candle at both ends. I made two visits to the emergency room, and then I was admitted to the hospital."

Physicians were mystified, first telling the superintendent that he had multiple sclerosis and then, after conducting more tests, that he'd possibly developed a brain tumor. They told him to prepare for the worst.

———————

Don Reimal
Independence Mayor

Long before Don Reimal was elected Independence Mayor, he worked to annex schools from the Kansas City School District in Western Independence. With his wife Jo Marie, he petitioned for annexation in 1974 because he believed educational quality in schools managed by the district there was poor.

Reimal, a commercial carpenter, began supporting political candidates whose agendas favored Western Independence after the 1974 annexation vote failed by a slim margin. In 1996, he was elected First District City Councilman to serve those neighborhoods. Running for Mayor in 2006, he made neighborhood improvement a priority with his campaign slogan "Preservation is Progress, Too."

"I tell people I am not a politician—I am an elected official. Politics is a game I don't like to play. I have a passion for people and progress," says Reimal.

His influence behind the scenes and in front of the public during the Independence School District boundary change efforts helped push the initiative over the top. With Jo Marie, he led a pro-annexation fundraising campaign. For the Extreme School Makeover he dispatched skilled city employees and equipment to help renovate the properties.

"Now that we've got the school district situation taken care of, people are anxious to get their kids in the Independence School District. We've got incentives for people to buy homes in that part of town," he says. One is the Missouri 353 tax abatement program; it offers tax relief to homeowners who make property improvements.

With City Hall support, the Independence Council for Economic Development has launched new programs to boost business growth. The first is a concept of sales tax reimbursement to "pay back" commercial property owners who reinvest in their property. Another gives up to $25,000 to franchisors who open a new location in Western Independence.

"The school boundary change and Extreme School Makeover really boosted our community. They inspired a lot of progress," Reimal says.

7

Mobilizing in the Heat

Van Horn High School in Western Independence had once been a vibrant public high school in the Kansas City School District that could have been stylized in TV shows about "typical" American teenagers. After it opened in 1955, booster club banners for Van Horn sports teams, called the Falcons, decorated hallways and classrooms.

Rick Sutcliffe was a big man on campus. As a Falcon, he won all-state honors in football, basketball and baseball. After graduating in 1974, he was recruited by Major League Baseball and won Rookie of the Year pitching for the Los Angeles Dodgers and, later, the Cy Young Award with the Chicago Cubs. Fans called him "The Red Baron."

But Sutcliffe avoided Van Horn for most of his 20-year pro baseball career. As a star pitcher, he'd donated souvenirs, awards and a Dodgers jersey to the school's alumni display, but after a few years they were stolen. On a visit to meet students and sign autographs Sutcliffe was processed through metal detectors installed by the Kansas City School District and patted down by its private security force to ensure he wasn't carrying a gun. "I wondered if I was at Van Horn or at a prison," he later would remark. The Red Baron never went back.

By 2007, the Van Horn that so many graduates cherished in happy memories was far different than when they roamed its hallways. "Van Horn looked almost like an abandoned factory," recalls Ira Anders, Independence School District board member. The metal detectors and security guards patrolling the halls, paid for by local tax revenues, were only the beginning. Ripped from hinges, locker doors gaped open. Double doors between hallways, called "crash doors" by fire departments, for some reason had locks on them, defeating their purpose should an emergency arise. Wires hung from broken light fixtures and fire alarms. The gym's wooden floor was splintered.

Most distressing was Van Horn's academic performance: evaluations ranked among Missouri's lowest and its dropout rate among the highest. In Sutcliffe's 1974 yearbook, photos showed 521 seniors. In 1984, there were 191 photos; in 1994, there were 77. Vandalism troubled nearby homeowners, including Melinda Littau. "I was very uncomfortable with the environment and I think the school kids felt uncomfortable or unsafe," she says. Fearing disruptive incidents, the Kansas City School District had eliminated many social events and even several sports activities. The athletic field and running track were overgrown with weeds.

Donna Pittman's deli and butcher shop, Curt's Famous Meats, is just a few blocks from Van Horn on Truman Road. "Even before I bought Curt's 20 years ago, families were moving out of Western Independence because they didn't want their kids to go to Van Horn," she says.

Curt's Famous Meats, a deli and butcher shop located on Truman Road near Van Horn High School in Western Independence, is one of many local businesses where citizens gathered to plan their involvement in pro-annexation activities. Proprietress Donna Pittman is an influential voice in community affairs whose customers include politicians, police officers, civic leaders and school administrators.

When word hit the streets in June 2007 that Senator Callahan successfully changed the school boundary law, a little bell on Curt's front door rang all day as people came in to celebrate and plan their moves as petitioners for annexation. They included Pittman's close friends: Eileen Weir of Progress Independence; Monte and Stacie Short, who lived near the Englewood Theatre; and Lois McDonald, who had opened a coffee shop on the Independence Square.

The man whose opinion everybody wanted to hear was Hinson who, very sick with respiratory distress, tried not to show it. Summer school was on. He kept up his office schedule and appearances at civic meetings, churches and neighborhood groups. His commitment to annexation, although cautious, and his statements about the petition drive, although neutral, gave everyone hope.

"Based on the information that we have presently, if the petition initiative occurs and the annexation issue is placed on the ballot, and if the voters of the Independence School District tell us they want annexation to occur, then we will pursue it with due diligence," Hinson told people. "We believe we have enough information at this point to know that if annexation occurs it will not be a detriment to the students of the Independence School District as it currently exists."

Officially, for Hinson and the Independence School District, that was all he could say or do. "We didn't get involved in promoting the petition process," he says. "I felt that it was a statutory process and if the district's patrons really wanted it to occur it was their responsibility. It would have been ill-advised for the school district to get involved in promoting the issue."

Blake Roberson, President of the district's Board of Education, adds, "We did not want to overstep our bounds. We didn't want to be seen as trying to take over another school district. We wanted it to be the will of the people and the will of the people wasn't only the seven members of our board."

Yet in his heart, Hinson was praying for the petition drive to succeed. Many of the appalling physical and academic conditions at Van Horn High were evident at nearby Nowlin Middle School, where metal detectors also had been installed. They were beginning to appear at some elementary schools in Western Independence and Sugar Creek controlled by the Kansas City School District.

Then, one evening in late July, unable to breathe, Hinson was rushed to a hospital by his wife. Doctors admitted him for five straight days of tests. He'd never been hospitalized before.

———————

On July 28, 2007, Senator Callahan stood in front of historic Independence Hall in Philadelphia, Pennsylvania, where he was attending a legislative seminar, when he received a cell phone call that helped change the destiny of the Independence School District. John Pinch, Deputy City Manager in Independence, told Callahan that petitions for gathering signatures to support the proposed ballot vote that, if passed, would allow the Independence School District to annex schools from the Kansas City School District, were ready for distribution.

Callahan looked at Independence Hall with its old, cracked Liberty Bell, a symbol of freedom for Americans—where the nation's founding fathers had written the Declaration of Independence and the Constitution. He was struck by the setting for Pinch's call, the place where government by the people and for the people was born.

"I called Pastor Bob Spradling of Maywood Baptist Church immediately and said, 'Contact everybody; we're going to have an organizational meeting and distribute petitions right away!'" That night Callahan flew back to Independence to set in motion the petition drive that, as he would later describe, set the stage for citizens in Western Independence "to be free."

His need was for speed and plenty of it. Otherwise, everything that he and others had put into the annexation initiative would crumble and community hopes for a brighter future would collapse. Steve Mauer had worked to ensure that petitions for use in Independence and, also, the Kansas City School District were legally compliant. He'd consulted with surveyors from the City of Independence appointed by Mayor Reimal to strictly define the school boundaries, so no contradictory claims could be made. Also, Mauer developed information packets and a PowerPoint presentation for appearances he planned to make at civic and church meetings to legally recruit petitioners.

Mauer did not officially notify his law partners at Bryan Cave that he was working *pro bono* and billing nothing for the services he rendered to the annexation effort. "It's not like the firm voted to approve it. I just did it," he says, grinning. "Sometimes it's easier to seek forgiveness than to ask permission."

As an attorney, Mauer was the Horsemen's liaison with the Jackson County Election Board, which serves Independence voters and others outside Kansas City's corporate limits. The Election Board had exacting requirements for putting any initiative on a public ballot. Its attorney, Bradley Constance, sat on the board of the Independence Chamber of Commerce; Mauer, as the Chamber's 2007 chairman, didn't have far to go to talk with him. Yet because of Election Board procedural dead-lines, only 17 days would be available for the petition drive.

The phrase "17 days ... 17 days ..." kept throbbing in Callahan's head as his commercial flight bounced through a particularly brutal thunderstorm on the trip back from Philadelphia. Under the new law, ten percent of voters in both the Independence and Kansas City School Districts who had voted for school board members in the preceding elec-tion had to petition in each district for a boundary change, and petitions for neighborhoods in each municipality had to be distributed to them.

Pastor Spradling was more than eager to host a meeting at May-wood Baptist to distribute blank petitions when Callahan got back to town. He was joyous and he thanked God for the chance. Through his interfaith prayer group, Spradling announced that the meeting would occur on Tuesday, July 31 in Maywood's basement fellowship hall. "I expected about 100 people to show up," Spradling says.

But on Tuesday, nearly 500 excited people arrived, filling May-wood's stained-glassed sanctuary. It was a touching sight for the pas-tor and Callahan: so many people from all walks of life, many of them young couples with children, many of them elderly and some of them disabled, moving with determination and smiles on their faces. As they entered the pews, they talked enthusiastically. Many bowed their heads to pray.

"It was an electrifying day," Spradling recalls. "We had an invo-cation and a benediction...Then I became an MC directing traffic." In clear, steady tones, Callahan gave instructions from the pulpit, ex-plaining how signatures could be solicited and that all volunteers must sign affidavits at the bottom of each 20-line petition in the presence of a notary after collecting signatures. The central task quickly became photocopying thousands of blank petition forms to give the gathering.

"Senator Callahan got both Kinko's and Office Depot running cop-ies, plus the copier in his office," Spradling says. "We had our copier at Maywood running overtime; it was so stressed that we actually turned down the air conditioning temperature and put a fan blowing cool air onto that copier. When we divided up the petitions into different groups and handed out assignments, it was a madhouse."

Hinson was touched by the outpouring of public support for the Independence School District when he learned the petition drive was underway. After five days in the hospital, with no definitive diagnosis and no certain cure for his mysterious illness, physicians sent him home with a "pic line" stuck in his bicep. Ruling out their initial diagnoses of multiple sclerosis and possible brain tumor, "they thought I had lyme disease and treated me for it, even though I didn't test positive for it," says Hinson. In its late stages, lyme disease can be disabling, causing paraplegia.

Nurses trained Hinson's wife, June, to use the pic line, a device that runs through an artery and stops near the heart, so she could intravenously administer antibiotics to him every 12 hours. He read reports about the petition kick-off in local newspapers.

On August 1, the first day of petitioning, the temperature in Independence hit 92 degrees; it got hotter in following days with constantly high humidity in one of Missouri's stormiest summers ever. Recruiting petitioners in all areas served by the Independence School District, in addition to neighborhoods near Maywood Baptist, was Callahan's main concern.

The Independence School District was one of five school districts that served students in the city, which measures 78 square miles. They included the Blue Springs, Fort Osage, Raytown and Kansas City School Districts, all operating in peripheral regions. The Independence School District served the central, oldest and biggest part of the community with 19 pre-K-12th grade schools.

"We thought there might be a challenge among Independence School District patrons whose children did not attend schools in Western Independence," Callahan says. He believed some might grumble *"You want to put something on the ballot that could potentially drag down school test scores, cost money and raise my taxes!"* But Callahan's volunteer petitioners encountered few such difficulties; many of them recruited other petitioners all over the city who fanned out in every direction.

Vaughn Cornish, a busy CPA and Independence Chamber of Commerce board member, says, "I wanted to get support for the initiative in the greater community and I found it." He recruited friends and even clients of his accounting firm to collect signatures.

At Matt's Medicine Shoppe in Sugar Creek, employees of pharmacist Matt Mallinson welcomed customers as signatories and recruited others as petitioners. Lois McDonald did the same at her coffee shop; so did Donna Pittman at her sandwich shop. Dennis Waits, the Jackson County legislator, legally could not collect petitions but drove his two nieces, Lindsey and Lauren, around the city so they could do so.

Jim Reynolds, a deacon at St. Ann's and St. Cyril's Catholic churches and his wife Lena collected signatures from parishioners at both churches. Sixty-eight-year-old Joe Bonine, a retired gas company serviceman, collected more than 200 signatures by knocking on doors near his home in Sugar Creek; only five people turned him down, including teachers in the Kansas City School District who feared being fired if they signed.

Callahan says, "I knew Joe as a constituent. He'd come to my office with a page of 20 signatures, then he'd come the next day with another full page. It was great, but I felt bad...he was tramping around in 100-degree heat."

––––––––––––

The law required a minimum of 2,000 valid signatures from voters in the Independence School District, plus 700 valid signatures from registered voters in the Kansas City School District, for the petitions to be authorized by the Jackson County Election Board.

Property owner Melinda Littau, a single woman with no children, thought to herself, "'If we didn't make this happen now, we might not get another opportunity for it.' I said to myself, 'By God, this thing is going to pass if I have anything to say about it.'" Littau's late mother had talked often about the Independence school annexation initiative that failed in 1974 by a narrow vote margin. So Melinda tackled her mission with gusto. For 15 years before she retired, Littau worked in sales with General Electric. In her quest, she put those skills, including quota-setting, to good use.

Before starting, she says, "I set goals for myself—20 signatures a day on weekdays, 30 signatures a day on weekends." She also dressed nicely. "If you are in sales," she points out, "you do want to look respectable. So, well, I *did* fix up a little bit."

Rather than walk door-to-door in 100-degree heat, Melinda, then age 54, loaded a three-legged kitchen stool that had belonged to her mother and a clipboard fat with petitions into her white, 1995 Buick Roadmaster sedan and cruised all over town, stopping where she knew people assembled.

During those humid afternoons and evenings, she set her stool in parking lots by entrances of almost every fraternal organization in Independence, from the American Legion Hall, to the Moose Lodge, to chapters of Veterans of Foreign Wars, and more. At Thriftway Grocery, Toys-R-Us, Cargo Largo and other retail stores, she did the same.

"I have lived in Independence my whole life," explains Littau, a graduate of Truman High School, class of 1972. "I saw how Independence neighborhoods in the Kansas City School District had declined. There was a big problem with a lot of kids dropping out of Van Horn High, and the schools in that part of town weren't physically maintained very well.

"I did not start off on that petition drive by saying, 'I think I can be the number one signature-getter.' I just figured, 'I can make an impact' and that's what I set out to do. So, I would sit on my stool in front of a store or somewhere, and when people walked by, I stood up with my clipboard...and then would give them my pitch."

Her targets included churches—but not just on Sundays. "Hey, people don't go to church just on Sundays. A lot have Wednesday night choir practices. So I would get in my car at night and cruise around the churches, looking for a crowd."

One of those trips found Littau at the First Baptist Church of Independence on Truman Road just as choir practice was letting out. "I chit-chatted with anyone who came out and I got to talking with the pastor and the choir director." Many in the choir signed her petitions and then something unusual happened. "The choir director, well, he talked to me about joining the choir," Littau admits. So she did.

In two weeks, Littau collected more than 600 signatures, far more than any other petitioner. *The Examiner* and the *Kansas City Star* showcased Littau in articles, and she was interviewed by ABC network affiliate KMBC-TV.

Before that happened, all petitions collected by scores of volunteers had to be inspected and notarized. Maywood Baptist Church was busy night and day. "My assistants Kathleen Wright, Penny Collins and De-Lois O'Bryant totally gave themselves to the petitions," says Pastor Spradling. "Kathleen notarized an enormous number; she stayed all day until 8 or 9 at night when things got hot and heavy." Wright, who was then age 70, says, "Our church became the center of activity for the petition drive and I was so grateful that we could be that center. I loved it. Every time I heard what was happening on radio and TV, I said, 'Thank you, God, for the opportunity you give us to help transform this community.'"

Callahan needed money, fast. On August 13, as the petition drive marched across Independence, he created "Kids Are Our Future" and registered the nonprofit entity with the Missouri Ethics Commission.[4]

"Kids Are Our Future" became a vehicle to promote the school boundary change vote and a basket for collecting cash to do it. Mike Butler, a local contractor, became its treasurer with help from his wife Denise, a bookkeeper.

"Senator Callahan started recruiting people for the committee," says Butler. "There were a *lot* of volunteers. People were saying, 'Put my name down; I want to help,' and, 'I have kids in the Kansas City School District but can't afford to move out—I want this annexation!' Butler opened a "Kids Are Our Future" bank account with $100 and the committee launched an Internet website.

A few days later, says Denise, "You couldn't go to a grocery store without someone saying, 'What's happening with all this, how are things going?" Outpourings of support rose across Independence and Sugar Creek as residents pledged to fight for positive change.

On August 21, four days after the petition drive ended, Callahan, Mayor Reimal, Steve Mauer and more than 100 proud citizens assembled at the Independence Chamber of Commerce to review the results. An astounding 10,065 signatures, nearly three times the amount required, had been gathered: 5,252 in the Independence School District and 4,811 in the Kansas City School District, an average of nearly 600 signatures per day.

Joyously, the party marched with cardboard boxes packed with petitions to the Jackson County Election Board headquarters a block away so the signatures could be verified. All were found to be valid.

Hinson, undergoing more medical tests for his illness but working in his office and at home, was elated by the news, "absolutely impressed" that school patrons had demonstrated their goals for annexation so passionately. The Independence School District Board of Education voted unanimously to officially put the boundary change issue on the November 6 ballot for local voters.

Missouri State Representative Ray Salva, who represented the Sugar Creek area, believed the Kansas City School District would fight the initiative. A few days later when a caravan of happy petitioners in cars, trucks and church buses drove to Kansas City to deliver copies of the validated petitions to district headquarters, the Kansas City School District proved him right.

———————————

Charley Dumsky
Jackson County Election Board Commissioner

Except for U.S. Army service in the 1950s, Charley Dumsky has never left Sugar Creek, where he was born in 1932. He was Sugar Creek Mayor from 1993 to 1999 after retiring as a quality control supervisor at Ford Motor Company's assembly plant in Kansas City, where Dumsky worked for 32 years. In 2000, he was appointed a Jackson County Election Board commissioner.

"Small town politics is interesting," says Dumsky. He describes Sugar Creek as a place where "everybody grew up together. We went to grade school together. We knew the mothers, fathers, aunts and uncles of all our friends."

When Dumsky was young, "the Kansas City School District was recognized as one of the finest school districts in the country," he says. But that changed after the Kansas City School District became embroiled in a desegregation lawsuit starting in the late 1970s.

When the Kansas City School District began busing students into Sugar Creek and busing local students to other schools miles away, "there was lots of animosity," Dumsky says. "Many people were nostalgic ... They wanted to go back to the neighborhood school concept."

As a Jackson County Election Board commissioner, Dumsky could not legally promote a local school boundary change petition. But Dumsky's many friends at the Kross Tavern where he drinks coffee every morning knew he favored annexation.

Dr. Jim Hinson appointed Dumsky to the Independence School District Transition Committee in November 2007, after local voters passed a school boundary change law enabling the Independence School District to annex local schools from the Kansas City School District. Dumsky became a Sugar Creek herald for annexation plans. He recruited support and registered volunteers for the Independence School District's Extreme School Makeover of July 2008. His wife Peggy, then 69, painted at Sugar Creek Elementary all day at the event.

"Many people got involved [in the annexation] because they believed it was a step in the right direction," Dumsky says. Before the annexation, "you could put a line through Sugar Creek and say 'This side is the Independence School District, and this is the Kansas City School District. But a home in the Independence School District was worth 20 percent more.

"The Independence School District is ranked very high," he continues. Dumsky believes that Sugar Creek real estate values will increase for that reason.

8

The Judge Agrees

"We've got to do better for those kids."

Janice Smith, mother, petitioner and fund-raiser

Janice Smith had paid for her children to attend parochial school rather than the Kansas City School District's Western Independence schools, and it was a financial strain. "Even though I am a Republican, Victor Callahan turned me into an Independent when he recruited me for 'Kids Are Our Future," she says with a quiet smile. "I got involved because I really do believe that kids are our future, and I didn't want other families to be challenged educationally, financially or emotionally like mine."

A Baptist, Smith attended Pastor Spradling's prayer groups at many churches regardless of denomination. "On one particular night, we all prayed for the school annexation. The ministers talked about our neighborhoods and how we wanted our children to be properly educated. The Kansas City School District wasn't even fully accredited! We were sitting in pews, and then we broke into groups and held hands. In our group there were about ten people. There were elderly people, young people with children, all kinds of different people. Well, it was pretty emotional for me.

"I'd never seen so many people like that pray for the kids. Maybe one or two people in the group had kids in the Kansas City School District, but the rest of us, we didn't. But we were all together, praying for those kids and our neighborhoods. It was like we all just knew, *'We've got to do better for those kids.'*"

Smith was among the high-spirited revelers on the Maywood Baptist Church bus in the caravan Callahan organized to deliver the 10,065 validated petitions to Kansas City School District headquarters on August 28. Callahan says, "We photocopied all the validated petitions because we did not want to give the originals to the Kansas City School District." The petition party convened at the Independence Chamber of Commerce. "I took the entourage to the Kansas City School District with boxes of petitions and it was incredible because when we arrived the media was all there. They were following this issue very closely and it was a big deal."

As Callahan, Steve Mauer and a group of revelers entered the gunmetal gray district headquarters building, all were processed through metal detectors. Smith was approached by a TV crew outside. "I had never been involved with anything like that before," she says. "I told the reporter, 'We are here because we want our children to attend neighborhood schools that are accredited, not partially accredited like the Kansas City School District.'"

Photo courtesy of *The Examiner.*

On August 21, 2007, four days after the petition drive for school boundary change ended, more than 100 proud citizens marched from the Independence Chamber of Commerce to deliver the petitions to Jackson County Election Board headquarters so the signatures could be verified. An astounding 10,065 signatures, nearly three times the amount required, had been gathered. All were found to be valid.

Inside, says Callahan, "We're all standing there, and we're waiting, waiting, waiting for twenty minutes, and while we're there *a fight breaks out* between two people in the lobby not related to our group, and the media guys start laughing, saying, 'This is just normal, day-to-day operations in the Kansas City School District!'

"Finally a lawyer for the school district came down from upstairs, and I made him sign a receipt in front of the TV cameras. I was following the state statute, and it was very important to have done it. We had to get the petitions to the Kansas City School District so the district would have the legal obligation to tell the election commission, 'We have received these petitions, and in accordance with the law, put [the annexation vote] on the ballot.'"

"Even if you have gathered all required petitions under the law, the Election Board wouldn't put a vote on a ballot until told to do so by the agency for which the election is going to be held," says attorney Mauer. In the lobby of Kansas City School District headquarters, he says, "We had the valid, certified petitions, with all the signatures satisfied under the law; we had the new law in effect; we had the Independence School District affirm for us, 'Yes, put annexation on the ballot,' and then the Kansas City School District said 'No, we're not going to do it.' They said, 'No.'"

It was a stunning moment for the crowd from Independence, "But that's what happened," says Mauer. Kansas City School District officials refused to accept the petitions that day because "they interpreted Missouri school district law to not apply to them. They believed their particular type of school district was not governed by Missouri school district law. I kid you not, when you got down to the brass tacks of their argument, it was: 'That law does not apply to us.'"

The next day, Mauer filed a writ of mandamus in Jackson County Circuit Court, Sixteenth Judicial Circuit, against the Kansas City School Board, the Jackson County Board of Election Commissioners and the Kansas City Board of Election Commissioners on behalf of concerned citizens in the Independence School District and the Kansas City School District. The plaintiffs were Barbara Burnett, Lois McDonald, Anthony Miller and Patricia Rector, who domiciled on both sides of the school boundary line.

"We sought an emergency hearing because, normally, when you file a lawsuit, a defendant has up to thirty days to respond," says Mauer. "Well, with thirty days, all the [Kansas City School Board, as defendant] had to do was nothing, and we would have lost [the election bid], because of Jackson County Election Board deadlines for ballot scheduling procedures." Judge W. Stephen Nixon, who was on a fishing trip when he learned of the emergency hearing request, agreed to hear the case within two weeks.

On September 10, when Mauer appeared before a packed Jackson County courtroom, its periphery was lined by newspaper reporters and TV camera crews. Crowds of onlookers, who couldn't get a seat, filled courthouse hallways. Paul Wrabec of Sugar Creek, escorting his 84-year-old mother Irene, had arrived early and sat with her in the front row.

"The courtroom was totally full," Wrabec says. "There were two sheriff's deputies at the door, one inside and one outside, for crowd control because this crowd was pretty wild, and they were upset because there were no seats left. If somebody got up to leave, the deputies would let somebody in. Everybody there was intimately involved with their heart and soul in the case because they had endured many bad experiences with the Kansas City School District over the last 20 or 30 years."

"From a lawyer's perspective," recalls Mauer, "it was one of those moments that you really live for." With scores of Independence citizens listening attentively, Mauer's plea before Judge Nixon cited in detail applicable state statutes and the newly-passed Senate bill chapter-and-verse as his rationale for requesting a decision favoring the plaintiffs. In retrospect, Mauer summarizes, "I said, 'Judge, undisputed, we have the petitions. The law is in effect. The election commission is here. The election commission says, 'If you give us the green light, it's on the ballot.' Here is the statute; we're entitled.'"

After listening to him, says Mauer, "The judge looked at the lawyers for the Kansas City School District and said to them, 'Okay, what part of this am I not understanding?'" Lawyers from the Husch Blackwell Sanders law firm representing the defendants "launched into 45 minutes, if not an hour, of argument about how the law that Senator Callahan had passed was inappropriate and that it violated the Missouri constitution," Mauer says, "and they made these arguments about how [the Kansas City School District officials] weren't governed by the school district law, and how they couldn't be forced to do this" boundary change.

Plaintiff Barbara Brunette, an Independence resident who had graduated from Van Horn High School and who enrolled her son in parochial schools rather than Kansas City schools in Western Independence, was in the crowded courtroom. After hearing the Kansas City School District's lawyers' arguments, she says, "It was clear they didn't have a leg to stand on...People weren't laughing out loud, but it really brought a grin to your face."

The Kansas City School Board's attorneys did argue with zeal in the case, but came up short. Judge Nixon's decision favored the plaintiffs. In his 15-page written judgment granting Writ of Mandamus on September 11, he cited applicable state statutes as they impacted the case at hand and acknowledged that the petitions were valid.

In his conclusions, Judge Nixon wrote: "Pursuant to Section 162.431, RSMo., Plaintiffs have a clear, unequivocal and specific right for the election to be called for November 6, 2007 ... Defendant, Kansas City School Board, has violated Section 162.431 RSMo. and its ministerial duty by refusing to certify the boundary change issue to the proper election boards to call the election ... Defendant, Kansas City School Board, is hereby ordered to call the election regarding the boundary change issue by certifying the ... issue to the appropriate election boards for a vote on the November 6, 2007 election.

"It is further ordered that Defendant, Jackson County Board of Election Commissioners, and Defendant, Kansas City Board of Election Commissioners, take all necessary steps to place the boundary change issue on the ballot for the November 6, 2007 election."

Rebuffed, the defendants' attorneys quickly appealed Judge Nixon's opinion in a filing with the Missouri Court of Appeals-Western District in Kansas City. But the Court of Appeals never acted to respond fully with a decision, Mauer says. This meant that the boundary change vote could appear on the November 6 ballot without further legal protest.

Once again, as occurred 12 weeks earlier when Governor Blunt signed the school boundary change statute into state law, revelers celebrated at the Courthouse Exchange on the Independence Square and at Ernie's Steak House in Sugar Creek, and for days afterward at Donna Pittman's shop and Lois McDonald's Main Street Coffee House. Mauer was elated with the verdict, particularly because he and attorney Megan Redmond from Bryan Cave had labored many hours preparing for the court hearing on exceptionally short notice.

A reflective Callahan, a hero in Independence after years of effort which had begun with people doubting his political intentions, borrowed a remark from late philosopher Arthur Schopenhauer to sum up his feelings: "All truth passes through three stages. First it is ridiculed. Second, it is violently opposed. Third, it is accepted as being self-evident." Immediately, the senator started planning a voter's drive for November 6.

Donna Pittman & Eileen Weir
Dynamic Duo

Donna Pittman and Eileen Weir may seem an unlikely dynamic duo. Donna owns Curt's Famous Meats in Western Independence where she wears gold-plated hoop earrings, a butcher's smock and a pixie smile when slicing beef or making oversized sandwiches. Eileen, a former public relations executive for the Kansas City Chiefs National Football League team, wears trendy fashions suitable for the wife of a regional bank vice president—which she is—and contributes a society column to *The Examiner*. The two often can be found cooking up plans for civic projects at Curt's in Western Independence.

Curt's is gossip central for customers and Donna is an insider for all things Independence. Eileen co-founded Progress Independence, which encourages informed citizenship; Donna is a board member. Throughout the initiative to gather pro-annexation petitions, promote the ballot for school boundary change and attract Extreme School Makeover volunteers, Eileen and Donna were vocal activists for the cause. When the Independence School District annexation finally succeeded, the little bell on Curt's front door chimed all day as people stopped in to celebrate.

Donna says, "Having those schools in the Independence School District now is pretty much the difference between night and day for the neighborhood business community."

"One of the amazing things," adds Eileen, "is that once the school annexation initiative got up and running, from the petition process right up to the first day of school, the energy level for this across the community never wavered, it stayed at a high level—and it's still at a high level."

This dynamic duo often socializes with other influential women who work in business, education and government, relying on each other to support causes where they can make a difference. Donna calls this all-female posse "Team Tiara."

9

The Ballot Party

"When he shared information with us, my soul just caught on fire."

Pastor Clarence Newton, Greater New Home Baptist Church

The Four Horsemen had seven weeks until the November 6 election. Not fully recovered but stronger after three hospital visits and two months of treatments for his mysterious illness, Hinson felt a profound sense of responsibility to achieve annexation for the Independence School District and its patrons. With annexation on the ballot, he was "extremely proud of our community, extremely motivated and, frankly, a little nervous," he says reflectively.

Hinson's conversations with district teachers and staff had convinced him that "they were very, very supportive of the annexation movement. I was *very* pleased with the receptive nature that all of our faculty and staff shared on this issue. They wanted to know how it was going to impact them. Would annexation hurt salary schedules? Or hurt our school district? That was easy to answer: No, it wouldn't hurt them at all."

All agreed that annexation would benefit students on the Kansas City side. But that didn't mean Hinson was not a little apprehensive. On October 14, teachers in the Kansas City School District vowed to fight annexation and their union began a heated, anti-boundary-change campaign.

With his right-hand man, Deputy Superintendent Dr. Brian Mitchell, Hinson set to work fine-tuning how the Independence School District would absorb more than 2,600 new students should annexation occur. But they knew very little about the true physical conditions of Kansas City School District schools and what might be required to sustain those facilities.

It was a busy, upbeat, edgy time for Hinson. "I was very pleased that we had gotten through the statutory amendment change and that the petition process was behind us," he says. With the annexation vote scheduled, "We finally had a date in mind when we might say either, 'This is going forward and we're going to make this happen!' Or 'It's over!' My feeling was that if people voted for it to occur, and obviously I wanted patrons in both school districts to approve, then we really had the green light that this is going to happen and we could get to work."

In the weeks before the November election, Hinson renewed his appearances at church groups, civic clubs, PTAs and other public forums. "I stood by available for all faculty and staff groups, all community organizations, and for anybody who wanted a presentation. "I didn't do anything intentionally to bring out the vote, such as knocking on doors to solicit support. I never made a presentation to a group asking them to go out and vote 'yes.' My presentations were informational; I explained the process in which we were involved."

Hinson's appearances inspired many people who saw him. Media coverage reflected Hinson's practical personality and earnest ways of serving district patrons. The Independence School District became a beacon of hope for many in the community, including the Reverend Clarence Newton, pastor of the Greater New Home Baptist Church, a primarily African-American congregation in a particularly poverty-stricken area of Western Independence. He had supported the petition drive and annexation from the moment he had learned about them from Pastor Spradling, and delivered the message to his flock from his pulpit. Pastor Newton had prayed with Hinson and Mauer at one of Pastor Spradling's interfaith prayer meetings, and Hinson made an appearance at Newton's church for Sunday services before the election.

"When he shared information with us," Pastor Newton says of Hinson, "my soul just caught on fire. We had people in our church really affected by the Kansas City School District. It really got to me when Dr. Hinson shared with us and he used a street by the name of Vermont as an example. I had church members who lived on both sides of Vermont Street. He said if you live on one side of Vermont, you're in the Independence School District and, on the other side, you go to the Kansas City School District, and he told us some percentages.

"I don't remember the exact percentage but it was, like, seven out of ten males in 12th grade on the Kansas City side of Vermont Street do not graduate but on the other side, in the Independence School District, it was just the opposite percentage. I was like 'Wow!' I started to picture families that lived on both sides of Vermont Street, and I could tell the difference, and that's what really made me get into the whole thing. I could see what Dr. Hinson was talking about.

"We assigned members of our congregation to help people register to vote. We wouldn't do it in our sanctuary; we did it downstairs. We got many signed up to vote, and we continued to announce what was going on from the pulpit and we were very much involved in the movement."

After learning the scope of The Four Horsemen's task, Pastor Newton began to pray for the men "every single day. They had a real job ahead of them. My wife Sandra and I, we made it a point to lift those guys up in prayer every single night."

The Four Horsemen wouldn't disagree that they needed all the help they could get. Callahan, Mauer and Pastor Spradling were brainstorming outreach strategies to generate a landslide annexation vote. Hinson was calculating the best way to absorb an increase of students that would grow the size and population of the Independence School District by 22 percent. The Butlers, along with other "Kids Are Our Future" volunteers, were working hard running a pro-vote fundraising campaign.

Mike Butler thinks it was either a goldfish bowl or a pickle jar. His wife Denise swears it was a cardboard box. Minute by minute it was filling up with cash and checks. The date was September 25, 2007, a warm Tuesday evening, and the place was Roper Stadium, also called Roper Field, one of the first lighted baseball diamonds in Jackson County, built in the 1950s on Carlisle Avenue near where Sugar Creek meets Western Independence.

"Kids Are Our Future" had announced a campaign rally for school boundary change. As the sun dipped low in the sky over Kansas City on the western horizon, the Roper parking lot swelled with cars, trucks, minivans, motorcycles and bicycles as people kept arriving with their children, their parents and grandparents.

"It wasn't meant to be a fundraiser per se," says Mike, "but a rally for recruiting volunteers to work phone banks, to place yard signs, to walk door-to-door with flyers. It was a hot dog supper with potato chips and soft drinks; KMBC-TV showed up and began shooting news footage.

"We were handing out pledge envelopes for people to take home. We didn't think people would give us money right there—then, well, people, starting taking money out of their pockets and writing checks.

So we put out a pickle jar or a fish bowl or something on a picnic table and people started filling it up with contributions." "It was a cardboard box," Denise asserts, "and we raised about $500 that night, thanks to people who donated."

Like mushrooms on fertile ground, little fundraising events began sprouting up across Western Independence as September turned into early October. "There were events all over the city," says Mike. "There could be two or three in one night at different social clubs, churches and just among different people. We showed up at them, or most of them, to get the money.

"Sometimes, we'd get a call at nine o'clock at night from somebody saying, 'Mike we just had a supper club meeting…' or 'We just had coffee with our neighbors and we have an envelope full of money for you!'" There might be five, ten, twenty or thirty dollars in each envelope. "We began to make deposits in the 'Kids Are Our Future' bank account every day. I didn't want that money sitting around our house!"

To help fund the annexation cause, Mayor Reimal, a graduate of Van Horn High, and his wife Jo Marie launched a pledge campaign directed to the Van Horn Alumni Club and, also, to people who had contributed to Reimal's 2006 mayoral campaign. "The Mayor and his wife sent out hundreds of letters with return envelopes labeled green," says Mike.

"Envelopes that came back with green labels meant the money was coming from alumni, as opposed to letters with black-labeled return envelopes, which we'd sent to people in general around the area. Every day the mailman would come to our house and first he would put out the regular mail we got, and then he would put out pledge envelopes people were mailing back.

"Monte Short [another Van Horn graduate] also was challenging alumni and people he knew in the business community. He would come by our house and hand over five or six checks at a time. It was amazing, the number of people who were contributing," says Mike. All the money

"Kids Are Our Future" raised went directly to paying for graphic design, printing, postage, yard signs, advertising, production of TV spots featuring residents who favored annexation and, also, TV air time, including on local cable television.

Appreciative of every penny, Callahan was thinking thousands, not hundreds, of dollars, and he demonstrated that he was a natural-born ad man. He knew that voters on different sides of the boundary between the Independence and Kansas City School Districts should receive different pro-annexation messages—flyers and letters that appealed to specific educational, emotional, cultural and neighborhood interests.

So Callahan produced campaign literature showing, for example, "kid-friendly" photos for Independence voters; other literature prepared for the Kansas City School District portrayed its Superintendent Anthony Amato adversely, ostensibly to connect with voters who did not support his leadership.

(At the same time, the Kansas City School District was running an aggressive, anti-annexation communications campaign managed by a nonprofit entity called "Save Our Schools" whose treasurer was a teacher in the district's schools. Its message, in part, argued that if annexation should occur, the Kansas City School District's tax base would shrink, its classes would get bigger and its schools would become overcrowded.)

"There were people in the Kansas City School District whom you had to worry about voting in the election, and the only way you could [influence] them was to offer variations of our message to reach them," Callahan admits. But the senator also had to make sure the pro-annexation message rang true among Independence voters and inspired them to go to the polls.

A bright idea presented itself. "Van Horn," he says, "had once been a great high school in the 1950s and '60s. A lot of people living in Independence remembered and enjoyed the nostalgia. The October before the election, I went to my twenty-fifth high school reunion at William

Chrisman High. I was thinking about the annexation campaign and said to myself, 'I've designed six different pieces of mail. I'm running out of ideas.' Then I looked at the faces of the people at the reunion. They were all enjoying the nostalgia of it all—and I thought 'Nostalgia!' 'Van Horn!' 'People over age 55 will remember Van Horn as great!'"

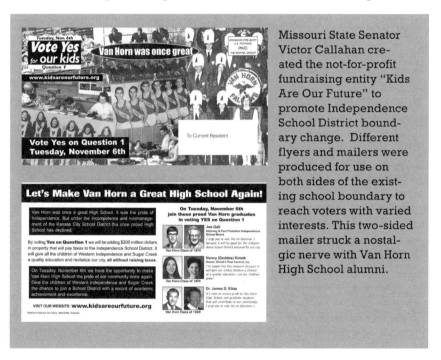

Missouri State Senator Victor Callahan created the not-for-profit fundraising entity "Kids Are Our Future" to promote Independence School District boundary change. Different flyers and mailers were produced for use on both sides of the existing school boundary to reach voters with varied interests. This two-sided mailer struck a nostalgic nerve with Van Horn High School alumni.

The next day Callahan directed graphic designers to create an oversized flyer featuring a collage of black-and-white photos of the Van Horn marching band, the Falcons football and basketball teams, cheerleaders with pom-poms and a chemistry lab, circa 1970, embellished with vintage yearbook photos and, beside them, current photos of Van Horn grads who endorsed the annexation vote. "Let's make Van Horn a Great High School Again!" ... "Vote Yes for Our Kids!" its headlines blared. That flyer was such a big hit, striking such a nostalgic nerve, that many voters who received it kept it as a souvenir.

Ask just about anybody associated with a school, a business or a civic association there to describe Independence and Sugar Creek, and you will hear that they are proud communities whose citizens preserve small town values and Midwestern ways of thinking. Deep traditions in local farming, tradecraft unions, family businesses, progressive education and an abundance of faith-based organizations are honored.

This may help explain the extraordinary volunteerism that arose in the final weeks before the election. "Being raised here, volunteering is a part of everything I remember, not just from my family, but from being involved at church, being involved at school," says Van Horn grad Denise Butler. "It was not uncommon for kids to always be involved in things to improve the community—from paper drives to going door-to-door to sell Girl Scout cookies. Whatever it was, you just got involved.

"This is a place where people came and could buy a home and start a family, and they developed a heart, an attitude, for giving back. It had to do with how we were raised—you don't 'do' just for yourself, you 'do' for somebody else, too. You look out for your community because you live in the middle of it. You make sure that your neighbor is doing well because it's your neighbor and, if he or she is doing well, then you are doing well. I think that around here, that attitude is a mindset."

Lois McDonald, a co-founder of the nonprofit community organization Progress Independence, calls Independence "a church town; a place where people are loyal to their faiths, but respect each other's faiths whether they are Baptists, Presbyterians, Methodists, Lutherans, Community of Christ, Catholic or whatever.

"It is a city steeped in Midwestern values of family, community and religion, which respects small-town ideals. This encourages people to reach out and help each other," she says.

Pastor Spradling, a witness to compassionate caring and charitable acts for decades, was extremely moved by the outpouring of faith-based support he saw as the drive to put annexation over the top for the Independence School District approached its zenith. "After the petition drive, local churches made more than 5,000 phone calls to help get out the vote," he says. "Those calls were made primarily by senior adult lady church members. There was a lady who was 89 years old who made 100 phone calls in three days and wrote me detailed notes on every phone call she made. It was exhilarating!"

As November 6 approached, both the *Kansas City Star* and *The Examiner* endorsed school boundary change. "For reasons that have become abundantly clear over decades" *The Examiner* editorialized, "this move should go through. It's about education." The Independence School District "has found ways to deliver solid programs and good schools despite limited resources...This district knows how to meet a challenge...This will improve education for kids in Western Independence and Sugar Creek. It won't raise taxes or alter attendance boundaries for current Independence schools. Over time, test scores and other measures of performance will rise in the [annexed] schools. Over time, families will feel confident enough in these schools to buy homes, move in and help a long-neglected part of town rebound."

Hoping the community's passion, hard work and concern for public education would impress one of the city's best-known citizens, Callahan approached lawyer and real estate developer Ken McClain, who served on the senator's educational task force in 2004. McClain, a successful attorney, had purchased and renovated many old, brick buildings near the Jackson County Courthouse on the Independence Square.

Callahan asked McClain for a generous contribution to support annexation. The father of six children who attended school in the Independence School District, McClain wrote a check for $25,000 payable to Callahan's senate campaign fund. The senator then transferred $50,000 from that fund to the "Kids Are Our Future" bank account, bringing the total donated for the annexation campaign to $87, 341.01. (In retrospect, Callahan says when he asked McClain if he would "match" the senator's own contribution, "I think Ken had in his head that it would be five or ten thousand dollars.")

On Election Day the polls opened at 6 a.m. on both sides of the school boundary line. The temperature stood at 33 degrees. A freezing wind blew all day, numbing faces, fingers and toes. But annexation supporters stood outside dozens of polling sites at churches, libraries and schools waving "Vote Yes!" signs on wooden sticks.

Voters like pharmacist Matt Mallinson, CPA Vaughn Cornish, Independence City Councilwoman Marcie Gragg, Sugar Creek Mayor Stan Salva, retired construction worker Earl Williamson and petitioner Melinda Littau turned out by the thousands, ebullient and excited, entering the voting booth to change their community's destiny.

At sunset, a crowd gathered around the Independence Square as Callahan, hatless, wearing a suit and tie but no overcoat despite the bitter cold, led a noisy vote-count rally. A live band played oldies rock and roll. So many people arrived that they filled the Courthouse Exchange and Lois McDonald's nearby coffee shop, spilling into the street where the senator, with a portable whiteboard, black-tip marker and a public address system, every few minutes answered his cell phone to receive updates from the Jackson County Election Board.

By 7:30 p.m., early returns showed that voters in Western Independence and Sugar Creek favored annexation by more than 15 to 1. When Callahan announced those results, the throng let out hoots, cheers and applause.

He introduced Steve Mauer, who was greeted with more cheers and applause from a swarm of people obviously enjoying themselves. Unaccustomed to such glorious public welcomes, Mauer, a huge grin across his face, waved at everyone.

Mayor Reimal, wearing a short windbreaker over his brawny torso, greeted everyone warmly, shaking hands all around. Tall and looking assured, stomping his feet in the chill, Pastor Spradling told everyone who greeted him, "Well, it's good to see *you, too!*"

Standing ramrod straight, hatless in the sharp wind, Jim Hinson seemed pensive upon his arrival; it would be hours before all the results were in. Yet as people approached him and introduced themselves, Hinson, too, smiled. "I hope we have reason to celebrate later tonight!" he said.

By 9:00 p.m. annexation was still unsettled. Whenever the Jackson County Election Board called Callahan with a report, he updated vote counts on a white presentation board. The crowd grew quiet as returns from Kansas City School District voters showed strong support for denying the initiative. Yet in the next 45 minutes all votes were tabulated and the ballot party exploded in merriment as those results changed history: More than 84 percent of voters in the Independence School District, 10,173 people, favored annexation. In the Kansas City School District 13,576 people, more than 65 percent of the voters did too.

As newspaper photographers closed in, Callahan and Mayor Reimal hastily unfurled a banner proclaiming "You're Free!" and waved it high over their heads. "This is truly overwhelming!" Callahan yelled, and called for Hinson to join them.

As cameras flashed, Callahan shouted to the ballot party "You made this happen!" Lois McDonald began hugging people all around, even as many jumped up and down. Mayor Reimal announced, "This is what we have been fighting for!"

Kelly Evenson, an *Examiner* reporter who'd tracked the annexation story for years, cornered Hinson for an interview. Thoughtful and calm, Hinson noted that the Independence School District's job was just beginning.

"We hope that this is a smooth process," he said, referring to absorbing the seven schools, determining their inventory and property value, hiring new teachers and, most importantly, serving more than 2,600 annexed students. He planned to soon meet with district teachers and staff, and also with residents across Western Independence and Sugar Creek.

"We want to listen to them and hear their issues," Hinson asserted. "We want to know what they need from us. Their participation is very important. There is a lot of work to be done," he told Evenson, "but we are excited for the kids and families. This is a great night for Independence."

Later Hinson told a friend that he was "elated, absolutely elated" with the election. It would be necessary to arrange a meeting with Anthony Amato, Superintendent of the Kansas City School District, but not right away.

"Intentionally, I did not contact Mr. Amato for several weeks," Hinson says. "One, I didn't want to be accused of 'rubbing the annexation in his face.' Two, I wanted to see if he would contact me first to say, 'The voters approved this. Let's go to work to make it happen.'" But Amato didn't contacted Hinson.

By mid-January, Amato was gone from the Kansas City School District, resigning after a fiery dispute with its Board of Education. By then, the Kansas City School District was planning its next legal moves, actions that would lead to angry standoffs between the two districts, delay annexation, breed confrontations and ultimately land both school districts in court. "Because the voters had spoken, I did not think that there would be such opposition," says Hinson.

Personally and professionally, year 2008 would become the most challenging in his life. For people across Independence, Sugar Creek and the Independence School District, it would be the most incredible year in local history.

Ken McClain
Financial Supporter

Over the last 14 years, attorney Ken McClain has in-vested more than $20 million to renovate 19 historic prop-erties around the Independence Square, the city center where Harry S. Truman once worked as an administrative judge. Victories in toxic liability lawsuits made McClain's law firm Humphrey, Farrington & McClain, P.C., very suc-cessful and enabled McClain to act on his commitments to community progress.

McClain and his wife Cindy have created well-appoint-ed restaurants, retail stores, a yoga studio, an art gallery, a gourmet shop and a first-run movie theatre called The Pharaoh, which is a living example of Art Deco architec-ture. These include the Courthouse Exchange restaurant patronized by politicians, and the pharmacy (now a coffee shop) where Truman worked as a teenager.

In 2007, McClain gave $25,000 to support the cam-paign to annex seven schools from the Kansas City School District to the Independence School District. All of Mc-

Clain's six children currently attend or graduated from Independence School District schools. Three of his older children were accepted into law school, "So I know they got a very fine education," he says. McClain calls the Independence School District "outstanding, with a wonderful infrastructure of administrators and staff" and "schools of distinction."

He credits Superintendent Jim Hinson with being "absolutely crucial" to the annexation. Many officials in the community doubted that the initiative would succeed because it had been tried and failed in the 1970s, says McClain.

"But Hinson stood up and said, 'We're going to do it.' He has been able to take what is here and improve on it, which is substantial.

"You hear such bad things about public schools everywhere and how public schools are failing. But I think the Independence School District ought to be put on a pedestal for what it has been able to accomplish, and I think the Independence School District can be a model for other districts."

10

Forging Ahead

"We knew there was trouble in paradise..."

Dr. Jim Hinson

"I knew from the lack of communication and correspondence from Anthony Amato after the election, and from his district's anti-annexation campaign, that the tone was being set for a fight," says Hinson. Yet the community was unaware of any imminent struggle. Rising tides of optimism spread across Sugar Creek and Western Independence as Hinson was beset with bad news that he feared might bottleneck the annexation or even wreck it.

Kent King, Commissioner of the Missouri Department of Elementary and Secondary Education (DESE), was someone Hinson hoped would support a smooth boundary change process. "Dr. King was an individual who would listen intently, gather all the information he could and then give his opinion and advice..."

But King had developed a malignant brain tumor; by January, he was less accessible. Then, Anthony Amato resigned after a fiery dispute with his Board of Education in mid-January, delaying crucial annexation dialogues.

Finally, Hinson met with Amato's interim replacement, Dr. John Martin, whom Hinson knew when Martin was Superintendent of the Grandview School District. "I knew John would shoot straight with me. I contacted him to ask if he would discuss the vote. He said, 'Of course.'"

Over lunch at Ophelia's restaurant on the Independence Square, "John's response was candid," says Hinson "He would be very willing to work with me on the annexation, but his Board of Education was in a different position. He said the Kansas City School District wasn't going to cooperate. He said, 'It's not going to happen.'"

The news was a major setback. "After that conversation the Independence School District Board of Education, by law, had to formally request that DESE appoint a Board of Arbitration to resolve differences between the two school districts," says Hinson, who had hoped to settle without arbitrators. "Our letter was sent in mid-January, but the first arbitration hearing wouldn't be held until late April," he says, recalling his frustration with the delay. "I don't think DESE was very excited about appointing a Board of Arbitration because it was an issue of very intense magnitude."

Pressing on so the district could welcome more than 2,600 additional students in August, Hinson, Brian Mitchell and district departmental directors attacked their responsibilities even though physical conditions and inventories of the Kansas City School District schools, and financial terms of the annexation, were unknowns.

Their tasks loomed colossal, starting with hiring more teachers. Dr. Mark Lee, Director of Human Resources for Certificated Staff, helped oversee this process.

"We received 3,000 applications for teaching positions from 15 states when the news spread across the country," says Hinson. "We engaged retired human resource directors from other school districts to help us with the screening process over several weeks. Every written application that we received was reviewed.

"Then we hosted a big event on a Saturday at district headquarters where some 600 applicants arrived for interviews. We also interviewed every teacher in the seven Kansas City School District schools who wanted to be considered." About 550 experienced new teachers and staff were hired in weeks ahead.

Hinson's team plowed through new challenges every day. The Kansas City School District initially refused to provide crucial information. For example, it did not identify the seven annexed schools' total number of enrolled students, those with limited English proficiency, those qualifying for free or reduced-cost lunches, or those in special education, nor did it release student health and immunization records. Despite such obstacles, "Dr. Mitchell and his team worked diligently to address facility needs, nutritional services, transportation, health services and all those issues we absolutely needed ready before opening schools in August," says Hinson.

"I don't think anyone outside our district will ever really understand the extent of our planning and preparation occurring at that time," asserts Hinson. "We were very detail-oriented in everything we did and had many contingency plans in place. Something like this had probably never happened at any school district in the country. We were very fortunate to have great departmental directors handling details. Bob Robinson, our Director of Facilities, had an enormous task on his hands.

"We were trying to assess conditions of the buildings, but initially were denied entry by the Kansas City School District to inspect them. Michelle Crumbaugh, Director of Nutritional Services, predicted the cooking and cafeteria equipment we might need, relying on information from vendors because she was not allowed inside the schools. John

Davies, Director of Transportation, mapped new bus routes, trying to assess how many children we'd pick up for the annexed high school, middle school and elementary schools. Our Executive Director of Technology, Dr. Gloria Stephenson, did the same for IT services, even though wiring, routers and servers at the Kansas City schools were unknowns. For all these contingencies and others, we developed Plans A, B, C and D based on what we knew, didn't know, and what we believed *might* happen."[5]

————————

On March 28, 2008, Hinson's father, Jimmie L. Hinson, died of heart failure after serving more than 21 years as pastor of the First Assembly of God Church in Carthage, Missouri. He was 75.

"That Friday morning," recalls Dr. Hinson, "I was in LaGuardia Airport in New York waiting to catch a plane to Kansas City when one of my sisters called and said frantically 'How quickly can you get here? Dad's dying.' I didn't make it back before he took his final breath," Hinson laments. "I was his oldest son. We had hunted together; we had fished together; we did everything together. He was my best friend. He was really my hero."

Hinson's father had encouraged him as a young man to choose a life path that reflected his son's own value systems, interests and passions. "When I was younger I spent several years working with my dad in his church, where I worked with the youth groups. When he had heart surgery, I assumed his ministerial duties for a time.

"This allowed me to see a greater perspective of needs that really exist in peoples' lives and struggles people go through on different levels. We had a young man in the church killed in a car wreck one night, just an ideal young man who was in college when it occurred. I still have one of his neckties that his folks gave me after he died.

"For a long time I was torn about what I should do with my life because people would tell me 'You know, you really should be a minister.'

But I felt that was not what I should do, even though it was the path my Dad had followed. I felt I had compassion for people and, with that, I felt education was what I should and wanted to do. So that is the course I followed, and it is where I found myself when Dad died."

His father's death was a personal tragedy amid extraordinary events surrounding Hinson, all underscored by his own mysterious illness. In October, a few weeks before the November vote, the Superintendent had checked into the Mayo Clinic in Rochester, Minnesota, "for every test possible," says Hinson. "The physicians said 'There is nothing wrong with you except one of two things. You have an unknown viral infection that may affect your health for months or years. Or, it's environmental.' I said, *"Environmental?"*

Some employees at Independence School District headquarters on Pleasant Street had developed symptoms like Hinson's. "That's when we brought in environmental specialists to test the administration building." They found that one building sector apparently was impacted by a mold, a bacteria or other unknown agent which blew though the HVAC system into Hinson's office and those of several employees.

In March 2008, two weeks before his father's death, the district ordered the building closed and relocated employees, furniture, systems and files to new quarters at 3225 South Noland Road. Everyone had four days to pack and go. Within a week, Hinson's respiratory symptoms began to subside somewhat; so did those of other affected employees.

This big move, his father's death and its grieving process, plus lack of cooperation from the Kansas City School District to provide vital information, spurred Hinson's determination to "do what's best for the kids" more powerfully than ever. He charged ahead.

The Four Horsemen convened to plan arbitration strategies. Hinson took the lead. Two DESE officials had told him that, based on legal precedent, the Independence School District would not be required to

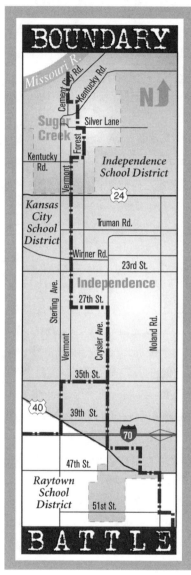

BOUNDARY

Missouri R.

Cement City Rd.

Kentucky Rd.

N↑

Sugar Creek

Silver Lane

Forest

Kentucky Rd.

Vermont

Independence School District

24

Kansas City School District

Truman Rd.

Winner Rd.

23rd St.

Independence

Sterling Ave.

27th St.

Vermont

Crysler Ave.

Noland Rd.

35th St.

40

39th St.

70

47th St.

Raytown School District

51st St.

BATTLE

For more than 50 years, a school district boundary line cut through the heart of Sugar Creek and Western Independence, dividing neighborhoods served by the Independence School District and the Kansas City School District. Starting in 2006, the boundary became the focus on a two-year struggle by residents of Sugar Creek and Western Independence. They fought to change the boundary so that the Independence School District could legally annex the Kansas City School District properties and serve students in seven schools that the Kansas City School District managed on the west side of the line.

Map illustration courtesy of *The Examiner.*

pay any money for Kansas City School District school property in the annexed area. The precedent was a 1986 decision in a dispute between the Portageville and New Madrid County School Districts in southeast Missouri. [The state statutes applied were 162.031 and 163.041 RSMo..]

Hinson explains, "In the autumn of 2007, before the election, Dr. Mitchell and I had met with Roger Dorson and Tom Quinn of DESE in the Independence School District offices. We specifically asked them relative to the Portageville-New Madrid case what might happen if we went to a Board of Arbitration in relation to facilities and cost. I wanted to know legal precedents in Missouri relating to any annexation.

"Tom Quinn had been involved in the Portageville-New Madrid case and knew all about it; he laid out everything that had happened. I was trying to determine where DESE might stand on the issue and, if our case went to arbitration, what type of ruling we might anticipate. They said the least of their concern would be us paying anything for facilities and for the transition, that we should anticipate not paying a thing. They based that on Portageville-New Madrid. They said, 'Don't worry about it.' I walked away feeling pretty good after that conversation."

Although encouraged, Hinson seriously doubted the Kansas City School District would simply turn over its property—and students—in Western Independence and Sugar Creek without a major fight. "Steve Mauer's legal team at Bryan Cave began preparing for arbitration from a legal perspective. We met countless times, early in the day, late at night and weekends, anticipating what might happen," Hinson says. The Kansas City School District might challenge the legality of the November election or bring other legal actions against the Independence School District. Hinson and Mauer also believed the Kansas City School District would mount a huge case for financial compensation or other reparations.

Dr. Mitchell's research had shown that annexation would be financially feasible for the Independence School District. In addition to new revenue from tax assessments in the annexed area, plus government funding based on student head counts and other criteria, the district would receive more than $300,000 annually from railroads for track rights-of-way.

Virtually all of those funds would be necessary to educate the more than 2,600 students arriving in annexation. (Mitchell's projections indicated that if funding formulas did not change, annexation would generate a small revenue surplus in four of the next five years for the Independence School District.)

With the transfer of school property and students, the Kansas City School District would lose such funds. Reflecting, Hinson says, "I think a considerable part of the issue for the Kansas City School District was about the money. They were generating money, obviously, not only from assessed valuations but from state and federal sources based on the number of students attending those schools. I think this was reflected in how hard Kansas City fought against annexation. Their balances had been dwindling. There had been deficit spending. They were trying to 'stop the bleeding.'

"I think they believed if they lost the Western Independence and Sugar Creek schools it would perpetuate or maybe expedite loss of revenue. But I believe there were two additional issues," Hinson says. "One, I believe, was fear that if annexation could happen in Western Independence and Sugar Creek, it could happen at other locations affecting the Kansas City School District. The third issue, I think, was pride and ego."

———————

Reporters on both sides of the school boundary began hounding Hinson, sometimes calling his office two or three times a day. With Elizabeth Streich, the district's Director of Community Relations, Hinson and Mitchell developed strategies for keeping teachers, the public and media informed. For assistance, the district engaged Lori Worth Smith, founder and president of Vibe Marketing Group, a boutique marketing and communications firm in Independence.

For any communications professional, consulting with the Independence School District during the most volatile, challenging and litigious period in its history would be a trial by fire. For Worth Smith, formerly an education major at Central Missouri State University, it became "a passion, a life-changing experience. I was wholly dedicated.

"Dr. Hinson knew intuitively how to handle the communications," she says. "He always stood on the platform 'What's best for kids.' The integrity was there; he never wavered: 'Tell the truth' … And that's what we did."

Early in spring 2008, Worth Smith's team began writing weekly "transition updates" for the district website after consulting with Hinson and Mitchell, to keep people notified about annexation plans and pending arbitration. The first arbitration hearing was set for April 24 in a meeting room at Union Station in downtown Kansas City. DESE had appointed three arbitrators: Randy Bryson, a property appraiser from Columbia; Mick Willis, an assistant superintendent in the St. Charles School District; and Dan Colgan, retired superintendent of the St. Joseph School District.

On April 9, Bryson and Colgan completed tours of the annexed schools. On April 21, Hinson announced pre-enrollment plans for K-12 students who would attend those schools. "We really looked forward to welcoming those new students and families and making the next school year a success," he says. "We began pre-enrollment so our district could better meet their needs."

At Bryan Cave, Mauer and his associates Jolletta Friesen and Jenny Deters often worked until wee hours vigilantly developing a legal brief with exhibits and documents that arbitrators wanted by April 22. This would amount to some 800 pages of detailed, organized valuations, inspection reports, debt analyses, property descriptions, maps, financial projections, economic data, state statute summations and copies of the *Portageville vs. New Madrid* decision.

During this period Mauer was sending emails at two or three o'clock in the morning, then showing up, looking refreshed, for morning meetings with Hinson to discuss details of the Independence School

District's apportionment proposal. "It was an extremely busy time for everybody," Mauer says. In Kansas City, attorneys Allan Hallquist and Hayley Hanson at the Husch Blackwell Sanders law firm toiled to prepare the Kansas City School District's proposal with Jeffrey St. Omer, that district's general counsel. It also totaled hundreds of pages. All parties anticipated a turbulent face-off during arbitration.

Stan Salva
Mayor of Sugar Creek

"I am a full-blooded Slovak," says Sugar Creek Mayor Stan Salva proudly. Six feet four inches tall, with blue-gray eyes and a full head of steely silver hair, Salva, age 71, was raised in Sugar Creek, a city of some 4,000 people on Independence's northwestern border.

Salva played a pivotal role in mobilizing local support for the Independence School District's annexation of seven schools from the Kansas City School District. "I firmly believe that this community is built around its schools and its churches," he says. "If you build healthy schools and churches you build a healthy community."

Most Sugar Creek residents are descendants of Eastern European immigrants who settled there early in the 20th century. Many sent their kids to parochial schools rather than local schools managed by the Kansas City School District.

"Ours is a very close-knit community," says Salva, who was elected mayor in 1999. "A lot of people thought annexation was a great idea that would never happen because the Kansas City School District was too big and too strong.

"Pastoral groups were a big influence in getting people in this area involved. People then started to demonstrate that they were willing to do whatever they had to do to support the cause. We supported it at Sugar Creek City Hall. We made petitions available. We promoted it in our newsletter *Sweet Talk* and on the city website. I collected petition signatures. So did Ron Martinovich, our city administrator. I think everybody in town was visited by petitioners!

"After the annexation, I was at Sugar Creek Elementary School with hundreds of volunteers painting, hauling brush and making other improvements. Sugar Creek city employees donated new plants and shrubs to the school.

"Everybody—*everybody*—pulled together to make this happen," Salva says. "People in Sugar Creek believed that annexation was a chance for us to help right some wrongs in our city. It was just amazing.

"This has been a very positive step."

11

Arbitration Delays

"I was fearful that the Board of Arbitration just wouldn't decide."

Steve Mauer, attorney

Rain and thunder pounded downtown Kansas City as dawn broke on Thursday, April 24. As the Board of Arbitration and those involved gathered in a meeting room at Union Station, they believed that no other arbitration of such magnitude had ever occurred in the history of public education in America.

In a soft voice, 62-year-old Board Chairman Dan Colgan announced, "We understand there is a lot of history and a lot of emotion in this case...If only the two districts could have gotten together this panel would not be necessary."

A green glow cast over the room as lighting dimmed to accommodate a presentation screen reflected off olive-colored walls. Furnishings were simple—secretarial chairs for all and folding tables. The mood was serious, Colgan's tones almost somber. He directed that each party would have one hour to present its argument, followed by questions, and then 15 minutes for summations. "This case is unusual because of the amount of property, the number of facilities involved and the number of students, teachers and families who are affected," he said.

It was indeed a face-off. Unlike some courtroom dramas where witnesses offer emotional, teary-eyed testimony, this was not a court case and the atmosphere was rigidly civilized. With Pastor Bob Spradling and Steve Mauer, Hinson sat at the center of a long table. Brian Mitchell, education consultant Chris Straub and other Independence team members sat behind them. Lawyers, Allan Hallquist and Hayley Hanson, with interim superintendent Dr. John Martin and Kansas City officials, filled a table facing Hinson and Mauer, eye-to-eye. The arbitrators, at a third table, could see both parties and the presentation screen.

Just ten feet separated them, but the Independence and Kansas City School Districts were $200 million apart. The Kansas City School District apparently wanted more than $157 million to settle the annexation, a sum the Independence team considered ludicrous. "In order to maintain the financial status quo and to continue to fully fund the (district's) bonds...and to appropriately adjust and apportion property and debt in accordance with statutory requirements, Kansas City School District must receive $157.29 million from Independence School District," its initial apportionment proposal demanded.[6]

The Independence School District sought $37.38 million to acquire and restock the annexed schools and to upgrade deteriorating mechanical systems, based on a formula to receive 6.3 percent of the Kansas City School District's total net worth, minus fair market value of the annexed school real estate. "This is fair...we have tried to be fair," Mauer assured the panel. To dispel any notion that the issue was a "land grab," Mauer reminded everyone that citizens in both districts had petitioned for annexation and voted overwhelmingly to make it happen. The Independence School District did not instigate the initiative.

"The atmosphere was cordial, yet tense," says Hinson. "Both sides were trying to determine the perspectives of the other. We were very prepared, but we were in front of an arbitration panel that didn't have much time to digest information about what was going on. We wanted to present our position as clearly and concisely as possible. We didn't fully know how Kansas City was going to present *its* position. There were unknown factors on all sides."

In their allotted one hour each, lawyers Mauer and Hallquist, attired in dark business suits, built pyramids of information—financial facts rising layer upon layer to support the points of their arguments. Meticulous descriptions of property assessments, maintenance costs, bond obligations and interpretations of state statutes were marked by gentlemanly allegations and disputes.

Hallquist accused Mauer of "double dipping" when he portrayed fiscal needs for the annexed schools. Mauer stated that deferred building maintenance costs of $23.4 million in the Independence School District's formula were, in fact, based on the Kansas City School District's very own assessments. A portrait emerged of annexed schools that had been neglected, of Kansas City patrons who wanted out of their system and an Independence School District eager to resolve the situation.

"All we are asking for are the buildings, the supplies and enough cash to make the buildings into a condition that the children need for a quality education experience," Mauer asserted. Hallquist argued that the Kansas City School District did not own legal title to the school properties; a related enterprise, the School District of Kansas City Building Corporation, did. That detail further complicated the entire issue.[7]

The panelists, at times, seemed confused. One referred to information in big binders the attorneys submitted as weighing "thirty pounds," noting he might realistically focus on "five percent" of it. When Pastor

Spradling was introduced, he described annexation as "a divorce," observing that voters in both districts wanted "to end our fifty-year relationship" and urged settlement based on the 6.3 percent formula.

When Hinson rose to speak he asserted passionately, "Our commitment is to our students and our families...We *will* do what's right by them." His ardor silenced the dim room.

As summations ended, an extraordinary thing happened: Colgan unexpectedly said, "I want the two superintendents to make a decision in terms of the future of the two school districts. I don't want the arbitration committee making that decision unless we have to."

The attorneys watched in stunned silence as Colgan continued. "I implore each of you as superintendents to sit down together before the 30th of April," he said. "We are requesting a written statement, due on the 30th of April signed by both superintendents that outlines an agreement around this arbitration hearing. I want a signed statement of agreement." He ordered Hinson and Martin to "hammer out a reasonable settlement to end these discussions once and for all."

For an instant, a tiny smile flashed across Hinson's face. But Martin did not seem so sure about Colgan's directive. He needed to consult with his Board of Education to determine if it would even consider the idea. However, on April 29, the two superintendents did meet, for hours, trying to resolve the impasse.

A frustrated Hinson emerged from that meeting and told reporters, "An agreement has not been reached in any shape, form or fashion. This will go back to the arbitration board..." By this time, the Kansas City School District wanted $90 million. Hinson had told Martin that he didn't want to pay anything at all.

Everything hinged on a decision from the panel. But five weeks passed before the second hearing occurred on May 30, this one at DESE

INDEPENDENCE ISSUES ARBITRATION UPDATE TO COMMUNITY

For more information:
Dr. Jim Hinson
Superintendent of Schools
Independence, Missouri Public School District
816-521-5300, Ext. 10054

FOR IMMEDIATE RELEASE – May 5, 2008

Independence, MO –

Independence School District Superintendent, Dr. Jim Hinson, issued letters to parents, faculty, and staff today updating the community of the most recent events occurring with arbitration. The letter mentions Hinson's meeting last Tuesday, April 29, with Kansas City School District Interim Superintendent, Dr. John Martin. Dr. Hinson met with Dr. Martin in an effort to reach a transition agreement independent of the Board of Arbitration. Dr. Hinson entered talks prepared to negotiate in the best interest of the children and families involved. No decision was made between the two superintendents, prompting the continuation of the arbitration proceedings by the Board of Arbitration, appointed by the Missouri State Board of Education.

Independence School District Administration will continue to represent their community and be resolute in their position of securing a fair agreement for residents of the area in question. "The citizens of Independence and Sugar Creek deserve to walk away with what is rightfully theirs," states Hinson. "These residents are entitled to reap the benefits of the tax revenue they have invested–tax revenue that should have gone into the maintenance and sustainability of these buildings and property. We are asking Kansas City to recognize this and expedite this process so we may get down to the business of educating these students." The state statute for the boundary change dictates "...an apportionment of real property, personal property, monies and indebtedness..."

The Kansas City School District did not pay for 5 of the buildings at the heart of this matter. They have been reaping recurring tax revenue from this area for many years but, in the eyes of many, have not adequately channeled these funds back into the maintenance of these buildings in Independence and Sugar Creek. Regardless of the outcome from arbitration, the Kansas City School District will collect $23.7 million in state revenue over the next two years for the Independence School District's students in this area, even though they will not be responsible for managing the education of the children who reside in this area.

The Independence School District is eager to execute this transition swiftly, so they may begin to better serve their new students and families in western Independence and Sugar Creek and provide them with a high-quality education.

The Independence School District communicated often with media and the community-at-large during the school boundary change initiative with press releases and postings on the district website. As the annexation issue became more volatile in the community, Superintendent Dr. Jim Hinson was hounded by print and broadcast media for comments, sometimes giving interviews to three or four different reporters every day.

headquarters in Jefferson City. The delay infuriated Hinson. The Independence School District was due to take over the annexed schools July 1 and start school August 18.

This holdup made Hinson and others believe the panel was not concerned about expediting a very important process impacting thousands of children. When he and Mauer arrived for the hearing, newspaper reporters and TV satellite trucks were waiting for them in the DESE parking lot.

"We anticipated that this second hearing would be very thorough and detailed," Hinson says. "We didn't necessarily anticipate a decision, but we thought it would address all the nuts and bolts of the issue with the exchange of a lot of information." But in the hearing room, nobody from the Kansas City School District was present except its lawyers. Only two members of the Board of Arbitration were there. The third dialed in by speakerphone.

The first hearing in April lasted fewer than three hours; this one lasted about 50 minutes. The panelists agreed to do three things: Review lease/purchase agreements with the School District of Kansas City Building Corporation; decide the buildings' value; and suggest how to apportion district fund balances. But they set no final deadline for a decision.

The hearing's most astounding outcome, in Hinson's mind: The panelists flatly rejected the *Portageville vs. New Madrid* case as a precedent for settling the matter. In that case, the state transferred property from one district to another without assigning value to the property.

"If we follow the previous case," Colgan told a reporter, "the Independence School District will be happy and Kansas City will not. If we do not follow the case, then Kansas City will be happy and Independence will not...We need to base our decision on information received, not by the decision made by a previous board of arbitration."

Hinson was appalled; Brian Mitchell was furious. DESE officials Roger Dorson and Tom Quinn had told them unequivocally that *Portageville vs. New Madrid* set a legal precedent that would apply in arbitration. But, now, the panelists and DESE attorney Mark Van Zandt claimed it didn't.[8]

Some members of the Independence team wondered what prompted this new position. Then, the panelists struck another blow: Even though the clock was ticking for the Independence School District to acquire, inspect, restock and reopen the annexed schools, they did not schedule a third hearing. "They told me, 'We'll get back to you,'" Hinson recalls. "That really dialed up the frustration level —*we had to get those schools ready for the kids.*"

A long, slow month went by before Hinson and Mauer received letters from DESE setting the third hearing for June 27 in Jefferson City.

"Our advance notice was just two or three days. The letter didn't request any information, but we were ready to testify, answer any questions and present any data that might be needed," Hinson says. "We certainly hoped there would be a decision. We were way past the point of being out of time."

Ira Anders and Ann Franklin, two Board of Education members, accompanied Hinson to Jefferson City where they met Mauer. "It was not a long hearing," says Hinson. "In my opinion, the decision had already been made. The Board of Arbitration tried to persuade everyone that they were still trying to decide what to do. Then they talked with each other about the settlement categories they had been considering. They verbally agreed and then asked their legal counsel to put everything in writing."

Hinson and his party were dismissed for lunch while the decision was written up. When they returned about an hour later, "We were given a copy of the draft document." Hinson claps his hands once for emphasis. "That was it."

Independence undeniably got the better end of the settlement; the arbitrators ruled the district should pay $13.7 million for the seven schools, one extra building and 80 acres of property. The Kansas City team had originally sought more than $157 million, later revised to about $90 million; now it would receive only a fraction.

"We jumped in the car and pushed the speed limit," Hinson says. "We had a press conference scheduled at Bingham Middle School in Independence for media that wanted our reaction."

Reporters and TV crews encircled Hinson as in bell-clear tones he declared satisfaction. "We knew neither school district would get everything they asked for," he said with a tight smile. The Independence School District was prepared to pay some form of financial consideration from the very start, he said. "I am happy a decision has finally been made. We are now ready to move forward." It was time to get moving and help the kids involved, he asserted.

Later, Hinson told a friend the district entered arbitration asking for much more than it expected to receive, much like a negotiation asking for the stars but settling for the moon. Yet he considered the panelist's decision to rule out *Portageville vs. New Madrid* "a striking blow because the DESE staff had told us it was applicable. At the end, I was just relieved there was a decision that was manageable so we could start getting the schools ready for our new students." But he was concerned about the schools' poor physical conditions and needs for costly renovation.

Mauer says, "I was pleased we finally got a decision. Arbitration had put the Independence School District in a tremendous time crunch by dragging on for so long." Janice Smith, fundraiser for "Kids Are Our Future," recalls "It would take a long time to get where we wanted to go, but I knew we could get there. I was excited for the kids."

One huge problem, the first of additional setbacks, emerged three days later when Hinson and Independence officials arrived to take possession and inspect the annexed schools. The Kansas City School District refused to let them in.

Steve Mauer
Dedicated Attorney

Steve Mauer, a youthful-looking attorney in the Kansas City, Missouri, office of law firm Bryan Cave, was drawn into the biggest *pro bono* commitment of his career because he supported the Independence School District annexation initiative. He also served as volunteer chairman of the Independence Chamber of Commerce.

Mauer participates in Chamber activities because his law firm represents the City of Independence in various matters. He routinely serves as a civic volunteer, although he lives in Overland Park, Kansas. In 2007, he worked with Missouri State Senator Victor Callahan to craft legislative bills that would enable a school boundary change vote.

When the Kansas City School District refused to accept pro-vote petitions, Mauer filed suit against the Kansas City School Board to force the district to put the annexation vote on the ballot. For months in 2007 and 2008, he responded successfully to multiple actions by the Kansas City School District as it fought annexation.

Except during arbitration hearings, he worked *pro bono,* logging hundreds of unbilled hours under intense media scrutiny. Yet the episode that remains foremost in Mauer's mind took place in June 2007 when he attended a gathering of ministers from 10 churches.

"I was there to explain what we wanted to do in the petition drive," Mauer says. "The meeting opened with a prayer, then about half-way through we stopped for a prayer. Then I explained everything, laid it all out, drafted a form of what the petitions would look like, and discussed what had to occur for people to be qualified circulators of petitions ...

"At the end, there was a final prayer. Pastor Clarence Newton of Greater New Home Baptist Church started praying away: 'Thank you, Jesus, for this day, thank you, Jesus, for the Independence School District, thank you, Jesus, for the doughnuts we have enjoyed here today and thank you, Jesus, for Steve Mauer.'

"I have been a lawyer a long time," says Mauer, "and that's the first 'Thank you, Jesus,' I ever got!"

12

Locked Out

> "We couldn't move anything. We couldn't mow the grass. We couldn't fix a thing."
>
> Bob Robinson, Independence School District Director of Facilities

"KC Rips Welcome Mat Out From Under School Officials," *The Examiner's* headline proclaimed. Steve Mauer characterizes the moment as "High Noon in Independence—like a standoff at the OK Corral." Hinson called it "absurd." Callahan declared it "a waste of taxpayers' money." It was supposed to be a joyous day for Independence, but by 11 a.m. on July 1 the temperature was 87 degrees and getting hotter as Independence officials were denied access to Van Horn High and Nowlin Middle School.

"It was as tense a moment as I've ever been involved with," Mauer says. At Nowlin, security guards from the Kansas City School District blocked entry to the school. More than 20 officers from the Independence Police Department stood by as officials from both districts glared angrily at each other. At Nowlin's locked front door momentum that had been escalating since the petition drive stopped abruptly. Police feared a confrontation.

Bob Robinson, Director of Facilities for the Independence School District, was livid with frustration. "I had a construction management company and an engineering services company we'd hired to tour the schools to inspect systems and see what needed to be fixed ... I had an alarm system company ... I wanted to change the locks when we took over the buildings. I had my people onsite. There was a lot we needed to do—but we couldn't get in. We couldn't move anything. We couldn't mow the grass. We couldn't fix a thing. I thought that we finally had an agreement with the Kansas City School District and everything was settled."

But it wasn't. The issues grew more complicated as the day wore on. Two days earlier the School District of Kansas City Building Corporation had filed for a temporarily restraining order in Jackson County Circuit Court to prevent Independence officials from entering, inspecting and beginning sorely needed renovations at the schools. A judge denied it, giving the all clear for building transfer on July 1. At first Kansas City officials let a few Independence people in, but then ordered all of them out. Robinson recalls, "I just shook my head in disbelief."

Mauer, who had hoped the transfer would go smoothly, was photographed in his shirtsleeves by *The Examiner* on Nowlin's front steps talking on his cell phone with Hinson, who was angry and incredulous. "The Kansas City School District was playing a game with us," Mauer says. "They were saying, 'Well, these buildings are actually owned by the School District of Kansas City Building Corporation.' So..."Mauer says with a lawyerly grin, "we played that game, too!"[9]

That afternoon, Mauer filed for a temporary restraining order against the Kansas City School District and its building corporation "to prevent them from keeping us out of the buildings." Word about the standoff was top news all over the region. Across Western Independence and Sugar Creek residents were enraged. The blogosphere exploded with angry criticism of the Kansas City School District.

Callahan called Missouri Commissioner of Education Kent King, who was still fighting a brain tumor, to urge that any state funds due the Kansas City School District be withheld until the Independence School District controlled the buildings. "This is a continuation of what we went through during the election," the senator complained to a reporter, adding that "Kansas City continues to demonstrate no regard for the education of children."

Hinson also called King personally to express ire with the delay. "I said, 'Commissioner, we have a decision from your Board of Arbitration that gives us possession of these buildings, but we are *not* being granted possession,'" Hinson says. "Commissioner King was *not* amused. He issued a public statement admonishing the Kansas City School District to fully cooperate with the decision of the Board of Arbitration and with the Independence School District, which they ignored." Instead, the Kansas City School District announced it was worried about utilities, insurance coverage and liability, a claim Hinson found ridiculous.

He told reporter Kelly Evenson on July 2, "At this point every day and every hour is extremely important to us. But, right now, Kansas City's position is that we cannot do *anything* to the structures....We already have insurance coverage for our employees, and our insurance company has been notified of the transfer." That the Kansas City School District would be liable for damages, Hinson said, "is just an absurd assumption."

King indeed reproached the Kansas City School District. He called for a quick end to its "delaying tactics ...This fight has already dragged on too long...In the interests of nearly 3,000 [annexed] students and their families, Kansas City needs to release the school buildings to Independence immediately." It was one of the commissioner's last public statements in a distinguished 44-year career. He died six months later at age 65.

NOWLIN MIDDLE SCHOOL

Photo courtesy of *The Examiner*.

This photo of attorney Steve Mauer locked out of Nowlin Middle School appeared in *The Examiner* on July 2, 2008 with the headline: "KC rips welcome mat out from under school officials." The Independence School District expected to take possession of the annexed buildings that day, but was denied by the Kansas City School District, prompting more delays and court proceedings.

In an editorial headline published July 2, the *Kansas City Star* implored the Kansas City School District to "Remember the Kids." After covering the annexation controversy for months, the newspaper began its editorial that day with the words "Schools exist for the benefit of children. Apparently, a few persons with influence in the Kansas City School District need to recall that lesson."

Recounting the standoff, the legal clashes, the arbitration and voters' desire for positive change, the editorial asserted, "This continued rancor is an unnecessary delay that threatens to harm the beginning of the school year for the children. Independence must be allowed access to the schools so classrooms can be readied. Taxpayers of both districts deserve a quick, fair resolution.

"The Kansas City School District would help its own public image by responsibly easing the transition for both districts. The provisionally accredited Kansas City School District, now reduced in size, should focus its attention on improving its own classrooms. The stalling hurts the children."

No one in the Independence School District needed to be reminded of that. Like an army wholly committed to victory, Independence officials attacked their increasing responsibilities *en masse* to ensure the annexed schools would open in good condition on August 18.

Simultaneously, they dealt with the "delaying tactics." The Kansas City School District wanted payment of millions of dollars immediately, although arbitrators had decided on the $13.7 million amount only five days earlier on June 27. Hinson had already engaged a bond financing firm; a meeting to discuss building transfer and other matters with Kansas City officials was set for Saturday, July 5.

Tension and pressures intensified. June 30 was the end of the fiscal year for the Independence School District. That meant Hinson, Brian Mitchell and other top district officials had to address other financial matters, too, including preparing two annual reports; one for fiscal, one for academic performance results. Hinson had appointed a Citizens Advisory & Transition Committee of 80 local residents to serve as a nonacademic support network and offer feedback about annexation. Email among committee members started flying and district telephones rang incessantly. Reporters begged for interviews.[10]

On Independence Day, Friday, July 4, Hinson almost missed local fireworks displays. He was preparing for the Saturday negotiations and his Monday court appearance to testify against the Kansas City School District in the temporary restraining order case Mauer had filed July 1.

"As a public official, as a rule I never talk about work with my wife and family because that would be irresponsible," says Hinson. He took a walk that night to collect his thoughts while his family slept.

On Saturday, July 5, in a meeting held at Husch Blackwell Sanders law firm offices, the Kansas City School District announced that it did not intend to comply with the Board of Arbitration decision. Instead, the district offered to sublease its school buildings to the Independence School District. Hinson, incensed, flatly rejected that on grounds that the lease could be cancelled by Kansas City at any time. Mauer thought the sublease offer was a ploy to "leverage more money."

In court on Monday, Hinson and Bob Robinson were cross-examined extensively by attorneys for the Kansas City School District and its building corporation. Hinson felt the entire question of entering the schools and making them ready for its new students hinged on the judge's decision, and he was very concerned.

He feared annexed school children and their families would be confused and upset if the Independence School District was denied access and thrust into new legal entanglements. Logistical considerations arising from such a scenario would be nightmarish: Could the district organize classrooms in alternative locations fast enough? Would students show up for class? Would occupation of the schools be delayed indefinitely? "Steve Mauer presented our case and also questioned us," says Hinson, "and I have to say Steve was very effective."

That afternoon, Judge Jack Grate ruled the Independence School District would suffer "immediate and irreparable harm" if its entry to the annexed schools was delayed any longer. He granted the temporary restraining order against the Kansas City School District, giving Independence unlimited access to all school buildings and their contents that very day.

Reporters lining courthouse corridors pounced on Hinson as he emerged from the courtroom. "We are pleased with the ruling," he said. "We hope the legal challenges will soon be over and we can put all this behind us and move on. In order to do what is best for the kids...this needs to happen."

Robinson, a big, soft-spoken man employed by the district for many years, was relieved—until he finally got inside the schools and was aghast at conditions at most of them. "They were just in extremely bad shape. There were holes in ceilings with ceramic tiles falling off some of the walls. Steam pipes were leaking. Toilets were broken and wouldn't flush. Partitions were in extremely bad shape—doors were entirely ripped off some of them. The floors looked liked they hadn't been stripped of wax in ten years, just filthy.

"Carpeting in some classrooms bubbled up where it had got wet and wasn't glued back down. There were fire code violations. Some of the 'panic doors' for emergency exit had dead-bolts on them. A bunch of elevators had been red-tagged for past-due inspections."

Robinson's team discovered pipes underneath the student media center at North Rock Creek/Korte Elementary School leaking raw sewage. Investigation later revealed they had been leaking for nearly two years. "We needed to fix a whole lot of things right away so school could open for those kids," Robinson says. So the district's facilities staff immediately began work on the huge task of interior repairs.

"We wanted to put those schools in the same condition that all the schools in other parts of our district were in," notes Susan Jones of the Board of Education, who also was shocked by the schools' condition. Was there enough time before classes started August 18?

Pastor Spradling of Maywood Baptist Church knew that Robinson's maintenance team needed more manpower to complete even minor cosmetic repairs before opening day, so he began helping Robinson recruit skilled volunteers to assess the schools' conditions. Spradling called one of his church members, Earl Williamson, a retired construction superintendent.

"There was a group of men at church who had good construction expertise, landscaping expertise and other skills," Williamson recalls. "Pastor Bob asked me, 'Will you go over to those schools and see what needs to be done?' That was the end of our short and sweet conversation because my answer was 'Of course!'" says Williamson, who was 70 years old at the time.

With Robinson's permission, "I went over to North Rock Creek/ Korte Elementary," says Williamson, "and went through the whole school building room by room. I felt like, 'Oh, my goodness, there is more work here than I ever thought there would be!' I made a list of things I thought should be done to get that school upgraded. To even get it presentable, it was a long list. Then I went to some of the retired gentlemen at our church and asked them to volunteer—there were about ten of us.

"For two weeks we went through that school patching, sanding, putting tape around woodwork and fixtures, electrical outlets and such so that the building could be painted. We pulled millions and millions of old staples out of the walls. You know, if a paint roller goes over a staple it bounces; the painting's no good and you've got to start over. So we did all that, maybe not eight hours a day but a few hours every day. The fellowship we enjoyed as volunteers was wonderful and we got a lot done!"

Earl Williamson's helpful group of "retired gentlemen" was, in fact, part of a larger expeditionary force in mid-July to assess conditions and plan improvements for the annexed schools. In military jargon, this was a benevolent commando unit that gathered intelligence for a major assault on the annexed schools to assure victory as the district prepared to welcome new students.

Some of its volunteers were part of the Citizens Advisory & Transition Committee Hinson had organized. Others were skilled craftsmen Callahan knew at the Greater Kansas City Building and Construction Trades Council, an affiliate of the AFL-CIO in Independence, including top officers David Kendrick and Gary Kemp. Still others, like Williamson, were recruited by Pastor Spradling or Bob Robinson, who was busy managing logistics and stockpiling resources for a very ambitious initiative.

This effort to assess conditions and make improvements was, in fact, part of an impressive plan. Earlier in the year, anticipating an enormous tactical mission to upgrade the annexed schools by opening day, the Citizens Advisory & Transition Committee had proposed an extraordinary idea: *Could we do an 'Extreme School Makeover'? Could we invite people and organizations to voluntarily pitch in to help fix our schools? Will people show up? Can we get this done? Can we make this happen?*

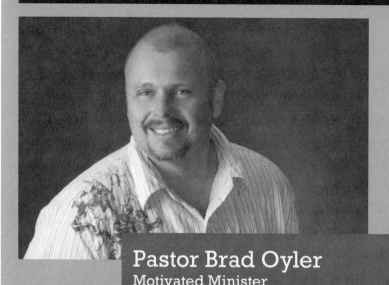

Pastor Brad Oyler
Motivated Minister

Every Sunday at 12:20 p.m., Pastor Brad Oyler stands in front of a white frame building in Western Independence to preach the gospel of Jesus Christ, using a bullhorn to summon his flock of alcoholics and drug addicts.

Pastor Oyler runs The Dream Center, an outreach ministry for homeless and addicted people that offers free food and used clothing. It is associated with the Englewood Assembly of God located nearby. A substance abuse counselor, he spends days and nights offering hope and the promise of salvation to disenfranchised people, most of them unemployed, some just out of prison. "My mission is wrapped around the homeless, the hungry and the hurting," he says.

In 1982, he graduated from high school "but I was an alcoholic," he says. "I smoked dope and I smoked 2½ packs of cigarettes a day. I could drink a fifth of tequila a day." In rural Nevada, Missouri in 1987, he visited "a little, rinky-dink church with old theatre seats. That's where I met the

Lord, Jesus Christ." He has not smoked a cigarette, ingested drugs, nor drunken beer or liquor since that day when, he says, "I gave my heart to Jesus."

More than 20 years later, Pastor Oyler experienced another revelation when he was recruited to manage the Extreme School Makeover at Van Horn High School to help rejuvenate schools annexed from the Kansas City School District. More than 800 volunteers worked at Van Horn, including graduates of Dream Center salvation programs.

"Before that happened, I never knew I had a desire or interest to reach beyond what I was doing with recovery and substance abuse counseling. But something awakened in me when I saw so many people working together to improve their schools and rebuild their neighborhoods. For me," he says "it is compassion and dedication to not only help homeless and hurting people, but to help the larger community.

13

Extreme School Makeover

> ## "We all came together to get it done. It was all about the kids."
>
> Barbara Burnette, Extreme School Makeover Volunteer

The Kansas City School District left behind clutter and disrepair when it finally, abruptly, abandoned the annexed schools just six weeks before opening day in Independence and Sugar Creek. Hinson and the Independence School District Board of Education would not celebrate annexation victory for the citizens of Western Independence and Sugar Creek without assuring safe, welcoming conditions at those schools.

"At the time, we didn't know when we could get into the buildings, but we had to prepare to welcome our new kids," Hinson says. Three months before the July 8 court decision forced the Kansas City School District to hand over the schools, Hinson and Mitchell started planning an "Extreme School Makeover" (ESM) to renovate, inside and out, six schools in one weekend with volunteer labor.

With little more than trust and determination, the Independence School District officially had begun spearheading the ESM effort late in April when Hinson and Mitchell enlisted a small management cadre. With arbitration unsettled, the district intended to conduct classes in churches and parochial schools for its new students if the Kansas City School District still controlled the schools by opening day. No one on the Independence team wanted that. "Yet we had no choice but to prepare for every contingency," Hinson says.

Pastor Spradling, along with Brian Mitchell and Bob Robinson, became *de facto* tactical commanders, reaching out for resources and able support. Independence Mayor Don Reimal and Stan Salva, Mayor of Sugar Creek, committed their influence. The district engaged Lori Worth Smith as ESM director, production supervisor, chief fundraiser and 24/7 media liaison. Worth Smith enlisted Pastor Brad Oyler of the Englewood Assembly of God Dream Center Ministry for homeless people as "school leader" for ESM management at Van Horn High, largest and shabbiest of the annexed schools. (Volunteers with top ESM roles were called "school leaders." They were assisted in a chain of command by "foremen" and "team leaders" at each school.)

On May 29, the management cadre gathered at V's Italiano Ristorante, a popular meeting spot in Independence, for a strategy session. The undertaking before them was huge, their deadline ridiculously tight. No one knew how much money and resources the ESM might require. Worth Smith recalls "We had no idea how many volunteers we might get—we thought if we had 800 or 1,000 that would be great!"

In the surge of planning that escalated after that meeting, Worth Smith was everywhere, from schools to city halls, businesses, churches, newspapers, TV stations and at her Vibe Marketing offices, night and day. She organized a steering committee of civic leaders who "knew how to get things done" to identify responsibilities and recruit more school leaders to manage foremen, team leaders and volunteers.

As this news flashed across the community, local pride and enthusiasm swelled. "Many people found hope for making progress where they didn't have it before," says Vaughn Cornish, a steering committee member who helped recruit volunteers. "It gave people new hope for our children, the schools and our community," says Pastor Spradling.

Tons of cash and resources were required: plaster, paint, brushes, masking tape, tools, screws, bolts, nuts, safety glasses, mops, buckets, brooms, cleaning fluids, ladders, work gloves, vacuum cleaners, drop cloths and trash bags for indoor tasks. For outdoor jobs: bulldozers, back-hoes, dump trucks, cement mix, giant garbage bins, driveway sealer, chain saws, wood chippers, picks, shovels, rakes, plants, mulch, flower bulbs, landscape supplies and tall ladders, plus experienced volunteer labor, were needed.

Senator Callahan invited David Kendrick, business manager for the Greater Kansas City Building Trades Council, to join the cause. "The group approached the construction and labor industry for expertise to handle certain projects," Kendrick says. "That started meetings we had with Dr. Hinson, Bob Robinson and Lori Worth Smith. We brought in some of our construction people willing to volunteer and divided up responsibilities among them. Then [after July 8] we went into the schools and analyzed what was needed so, at the Extreme School Makeover, our people would know what to do."

As planning advanced, Vibe's sponsorship outreach clicked into high gear. Worth Smith's team produced a package that offered corporations advertising exposure, T-shirts, website links and signage options for financial donations. Within two months, more than $116,000 in cash and $432,000 in supplies, labor and media co-sponsorships had been committed.

"We had several drop-off points for donations. Pallets of donated supplies began piling up at the school district central office," Worth

Smith says. "If we got a big donation of supplies, Bob Robinson and his team got it with a truck."

Marshalling resources would have been impossible without committed co-leaders who attended weekly planning sessions. School leaders with overall ESM site responsibility were appointed for each school. More than 30 foremen and team leaders, at least five per school, were recruited to manage volunteers for the registration booths, painting, cleaning, repair and landscaping jobs. Vibe produced ESM "how to" kits worthy of a military operation (Appendix) including sketches of the schools, rooms and grounds provided by Bob Robinson, with detailed instructions for handling ESM tasks.

Robinson scrounged essential supplies and materials not covered by donations or sponsors. Former U.S. Air Force jet pilot Tony Durant, volunteer foreman at Three Trails Elementary School, recalls, "Team leaders and foremen went to planning meetings where Bob would say, 'Tell me what you need equipment-wise, and we'll get it.'

"I needed a bunch of Plexiglas and hundreds of screws, nuts and bolts to replace exterior door panels all fogged up. I asked Bob, 'Can you find all this?' Sure enough, he tracked everything down ...he even had the Plexiglas cut to the right sizes and ready to go!"

Durant also needed 40 gallons of special paint for striping playgrounds, parking lots and curbs. "Three Trails' playground was so worn," he says, "you couldn't see stripes for the basketball keys and dodge-ball circles.

"I went to Don Sladek at Sladek-Do-It-Best Hardware and asked, 'Can you provide a little paint?' He said, 'Heck, I've got a parking lot striping machine; you can use that,' and he also ended up donating all the paint, about eight hundred bucks worth!"

Stories like these inspired everyone involved as ESM weekend neared. "Everybody was fired up!" says Deacon Jim Reynolds of St. Ann's and St. Cyril's' Catholic churches.

"A lot of folks had pre-registered, so we knew there would be a good turnout," says Durant. In fact, people in Kansas, Illinois, Iowa, Missouri, Nebraska and Oklahoma who'd attended the annexed schools years earlier signed up to come back as volunteers.

Matt Mallinson, school leader for Sugar Creek Elementary ESM, says, "We prepared a list of everything to be done and knew what we wanted to accomplish. It was a very exciting time." He was assisted by Kendrick, who also advised other school leaders and served as foreman at the Sugar Creek Elementary ESM. Worth Smith's list of businesses, religious and labor officials, and families who rendered crucial backing includes hundreds of names. But she reserves special praise for the thousands of people who volunteered for ESM tasks with goodness in their hearts. So many that, five days before the event, Worth Smith's staff had to cease formal pre-registration, stop mailing confirmation letters and personally contact people to discuss their assignments—Vibe made 800 phone calls.

"That week, I got a little emotional, realizing that huge numbers of people were committing to help," Worth Smith says. The night before ESM weekend, "I didn't want to go to sleep—I *couldn't* sleep. Everything was ready, all coming to a head. I had a gazillion things going through my mind: 'Will everything go smoothly?'...' Will the food arrive on time?'...'Will registration be OK?'...' Did we get all the materials we need?'"

That night, before setting his alarm clock for 5 a.m., Hinson reflected on the extraordinary activities of the previous 18 months. He realized, "This is really about democracy. It's about people who hoped for a different way of life and wanted a different educational environment to rebuild their schools and community. They did it with a petition process and a voting process. They had gotten to a point where they said: 'We want a change. Here is what we want.'—and then they did it for themselves, their children and families."

Says Hinson: "Throughout the initiative I witnessed passion from people on a daily basis. Everything was being accomplished by committed people and teams of volunteers. It was amazing and tremendously gratifying for me and the Independence School District to see and be part of it."

At dawn the next morning church steeples across Independence and Sugar Creek glowed as sun rays crossed their spires. The first light was serene, the sky a peaceful blue and the air typical for Missouri in July: sweltering. At the annexed schools, school leaders, foremen and team leaders gathered at 6:30 a.m., eager to begin.

Pastor Spradling, school leader at North Rock Creek/Korte Elementary School, with his foreman Maywood Baptist Church member Earl Williamson, bowed his head for a prayer of thanks and offered blessings for a perfect day. More than 300 Maywood Baptist members had volunteered.

Hinson, Callahan, Worth Smith and Mayor Reimal showed up early at Nowlin Middle School to prepare for opening ceremonies. Precisely at 8 a.m., a troop of Boy Scouts dressed in their summer regalia of shoulder sashes and merit badges raised the Stars and Stripes up a flagpole as more than 600 moms, dads, grandmas, grandpas, friends, neighbors and students began singing the National Anthem. Worth Smith was not alone with tears in her eyes as their voices reached higher with the words *"What so proudly we hail ..."* and the crowd burst into cheers at the anthem's end, a joyful sound that resonated across Nowlin's grassy lawn.

The roar of engines thundered as a color guard of Harley-Davidson motorcycle riders rumbled proudly into the school driveways officially kicking off the activities. The Extreme School Makeover was definitely on!

Photo courtesy of *The Examiner.*

After months of setbacks for the Independence School District, nearly 3,000 volunteers participated in an inspiring Extreme School Makeover on July 26 and 27, 2008, to help renovate six schools annexed by the District. Skilled craftsmen from trade unions volunteered with people from all walks of life to prepare the schools for opening day and welcome new students to the Independence School District.

Photo courtesy of *The Examiner.*

Photo courtesy of *The Examiner.*

Quickly it became evident that this incredible event was about truly more than fixing up long-neglected schools. For many volunteers, it seemed they had lost something in their lives and found it again, or wanted to find it, in the elementary school classrooms or in Van Horn hallways where they'd grown up. It was something promising, uplifting and somehow spiritual. It simultaneously dovetailed past and present with future goals wholly worthwhile.

Eileen Weir "wouldn't miss it for the world." She hurried back from a Colorado trip to volunteer at Nowlin Middle School because, "This is my neighborhood, this is where my family lives," she says. "It was a beautiful thing to be involved in, a very rewarding experience after we'd worked so hard for years to reclaim those schools."

At Three Trails Elementary, Lysle Weeks, the school leader, couldn't believe the turnout. There, as at every school, many people who had not pre-registered simply showed up with shovels, paintbrushes, buckets and tools, ready to help. At Nowlin Middle School, an elderly woman too arthritic to stand straight or bend, painted walls between knee and shoulder height.

At North Rock Creek/Korte Elementary, 70-year-old Louise Douglas, too frail to work, insisted on being escorted into every classroom, stairwell, lavatory, office and closet so she could pray for the children, teachers and administrators. One man canceled his cancer chemotherapy that weekend to volunteer. (A few weeks later, he died.)

Carpenters, plumbers, bricklayers, cement workers and craftsmen from 17 trade unions showed up with their toolboxes to render expertise; so did city employees from Independence and Sugar Creek who operated dump trucks and landscape equipment. Corporate executives, doctors, lawyers, dentists and college professors wearing T-shirts and shorts arrived with spouses and children. With a $900,000 bucket truck, Independence Fire Department firefighters repainted the school flagpoles.

Paul Wrabec was stunned by Sugar Creek Elementary's condition. "I used to walk to school. I hadn't been back since seventh grade, and I was real disappointed at how it was kept by the Kansas City School District. What a mess! Then I began recalling the great times I had there ... you know, being on the playground."

All day Saturday Wrabec wire-brushed peeling paint from playground tables and then repainted them; on Sunday he was back with a chainsaw to cut trees and load brush into dump trucks. For Wrabec, a landlord, the ESM had another special meaning: "With Sugar Creek now in the Independence School District, families with children wanted to rent my properties. They didn't want to do that when the Kansas City School District operated the school."

At Van Horn, more than 825 people turned out on Saturday to scrub floors, replace woodwork, fix broken windows, paint walls, ceilings and staircases, trim trees, landscape the grounds, pour new concrete, install new fences, remove the old scoreboard, haul away garbage and recycle junk. "It was incredible to walk down a hallway and see fifty people painting, really going at it—everybody was really *working*," says Steve Mauer, who ended his day splattered with paint and dust.

"We worked from sun up to sun down," says Pastor Oyler, who found the experience "simply incredible." On Sunday afternoon, hundreds returned. "We had every age group except young children working, and it was the most amazing experience. I remember one lady who wasn't sure what to do. I told her, 'You've got to be a team leader,' and she said, 'I am not a leader, I am a worker,' and I said, 'I need you to be a leader right now.'

"At the end of the day she came back to me and said, 'I never realized I could do this. I thought I would be a better worker than a leader.' But, you know, she showed her leadership potential and, with that experience, she awakened to those capabilities. She never really knew all the strength she had inside."

By late afternoon Sunday, the tally was in: damage and defects in more than 180 classrooms and offices at six schools had been repaired. Every room smelled of new paint. The metal detectors at Van Horn and Nowlin were gone. Gym floors, bleachers and scoreboards were updated. Playground equipment was set up.

Hundreds of new trees, shrubs and flower beds were embedded, mulched and watered. New concrete sidewalks and curbs were poured. Potholes were fixed. Scores of old fence posts in concrete footings had been dug up, hauled away or replaced. New signage was in place. Tons of garbage and debris were disposed of. The schools were spotless.

"Over 3,000 people volunteered to work—it was unbelievable!" says Worth Smith. Media sprang on administrators and teachers for comments. Michelle Paulsen, a second-grade teacher at Three Trails, summed up many feelings: "I am humbled. This is just indescribable that all of these people turned out to do this ...".

Ken Johnston of the Board of Education called it "a miracle" and "overwhelming." Charley Dumsky, former Mayor of Sugar Creek, called the outpouring "The experience of a lifetime."

Hinson told reporters, who considered the ESM one of the biggest, most inspiring stories in local history, "I've never seen anything like this in all my years as an educator." But then he was surprised by something totally unexpected: Volunteers approached Hinson at day's end and told him they wanted to come back. Many offered to return before opening day to "touch things up." The Independence Garden Club wanted to nurture new plants. Dolores Faherty, a woman in her 80s, vowed to visit Van Horn twice a week to dust offices and window blinds—and she did.

At the end of ESM weekend, exhausted, Worth Smith went home to the arms of her children. "I woke up the next day and just started writing 'thank you' letters, crying and writing. I felt so lucky and blessed. An amazing thing had happened, and I felt very small; I was humbled by the humanity and compassion people had showed.

"Really, I had withdrawals from the Extreme School Makeover for about three weeks. It was like, 'Now what do I do? I spent a lot of time soul-searching. I started touring local churches with my mom, different churches. We would sit and listen. I didn't want to let go of the community."

For Pastor Oyler, being Van Horn's school leader was an awakening. "The experience inspired a vision within me of what people can achieve together. Once you catch that vision and let compassion pour into you—for this, it *was 'Let's do this for our school children...Let's do this for our city'*—then you can be more of a citizen, connect more with a community and help the rest of society."

Hinson and the Independence School District Board of Education immediately began planning a banquet for August 11 to thank all volunteers and sponsors who enabled such enormous success. Pastor Spradling of Maywood Baptist and Pastor Brian Ross of Englewood Assembly of God scheduled special Sunday services to express gratitude for labor and civic organizations that contributed so much.

The Four Horsemen knew the petition drive, boundary change vote, arbitration, court hearings and the Extreme School Makeover were not an end, but a beginning—a platform for more educational progress and community achievement. As Hinson arrived home that Sunday evening with his wife, he said, "With a community like this, I think the best is yet to come."

Lori Worth Smith
Marketing Visionary

The Extreme School Makeover is a stellar example of cause-related community action. Cheerful, enthusiastic Lori Worth Smith and her firm, Vibe Marketing Group, were engaged by the Independence School District to help organize the event with planning, advertising, creative services, media relations, fundraising and logistical support. Vibe did it "with plenty of other peoples' help," she asserts.

"First, we developed an Extreme School Makeover logo to generate awareness." Those colorful logos started appearing in Independence School District newsletters and web pages with the tagline *"Lifting Hammers, Lifting Spirits"* or *"Make an Extreme Difference."*

Soon, churches and civic associations featured those logos with Extreme School Makeover announcements in their websites and newsletters. Worth Smith also organized a steering committee of civic leaders and developed a formal marketing plan.

"We outlined how we would get the word out...our goals for the event...how we would recruit volunteers and how we would handle volunteer registrations. We created an online registration form for the Independence School District website." It soon appeared on many other civic websites. "Then we did mailings inviting people to 'Send us your application or go online, tell us how you want to work on Extreme School Makeover weekend.'"

Vibe launched a "Get Involved" ad campaign and, also, a fundraising campaign that raised more than $550,000 in cash, labor, supplies and media co-sponsorships. (Appendix). The firm developed a detailed "how-to kit" for volunteer leaders with input from district officials.

Worth Smith worked 12 to 15 hours a day to help organize the triumphant event. "It was very emotional for me, I was moved by so many people's involvement," she says.

She continues to help manage "mini-makeovers" at local parks and schools and Vibe organized "Project Shine" for the district in summer 2009. Recently, Worth Smith was named Executive Director for the School District of Independence Foundation, a part-time role she loves. "It's *fabulous*," she asserts with a big smile.

14

Celebrating the Future: Lessons Learned

"The Independence School District makes us feel like we're all part of one community."

Ron Martinovich - Sugar Creek City Administrator

Backpack slung over his shoulder, a wide-eyed boy walked through Van Horn High's glass front doors on opening day August 18, 2008, and looked at the blur of students in the foyer. He blinked, slowly turned, looking left and right. Then he spun around, paced out the doors, spun again and stepped back inside.

Ken Johnston, an Independence School District board member, saw the boy and said, "Welcome to Van Horn. How's everything going?" The teenager looked up and said, "I can't believe the metal detectors are gone." Then he disappeared down the noisy hallway to join his classmates.

"To me that indicated the Independence School District made positive impressions on our new students the minute we opened our doors after the annexation," says Johnston.

But the Independence School District did far more than just make a good first impression. For the school year that ended May 2009, 64 percent of Van Horn students scored at "proficient or advanced" levels in state academic evaluations of reading skills—a 400 percent improvement over previous-year results of 16 percent for Van Horn students under the Kansas City regime. Those preliminary test scores also showed nearly doubled proficiency in math and biology.

Patrick Layden, Van Horn social studies teacher and teaching coach, says, "Test scores like that reaffirm my belief in a public school system's power to change the outlook and performance of kids for the better. When students feel they are cared about, they perform better and will do almost anything they are asked to do. If they feel they are not valued as people—that they are just 'a number' in a school system and that teachers don't want to help them—then their activity and outlook reflects how they feel and they don't perform well."

After nine years teaching at William Chrisman High School across town, Layden requested a transfer to Van Horn to help students at the school's inaugural year in the Independence School District. "I really do believe a school district is the single most important institution for bringing together a community's identity and spirit of unity," says Layden. "The people of Western Independence and Sugar Creek rose up to redefine their kids' educational future by pursuing annexation. That would not have happened if they didn't believe the district they were coming to, the Independence School District, was a much better option."

Jana Waits, Independence School District board member, concurs. "The school boundary change marked a whole new beginning for people who wanted a transformation. They found a school district full of people who care about them, who believe in them and who work to offer new educational opportunities. We're really talking about helping whole families."[11]

At Van Horn, the Independence School District provides 15 extra-curricular and athletic activities not available to students in the Kansas City School District in recent years, in addition to award-winning academic programs. For example: Layden was appalled to learn that Van Horn didn't have a Student Council. "So I approached Principal Dr. Greg Netzer who was 110 percent in favor of having one." Layden discussed the concept with groups of students, who subsequently elected class and school-wide Student Council officers.

Other students, with faculty support, began planning Van Horn's 2008 Homecoming celebration, an event cancelled the previous year by the Kansas City School District. Rousing Homecoming festivities in October featured a boisterous parade in Western Independence with vibrant Van Horn red and gray floats, the Falcons' marching band, and antique fire trucks clanging their bells. "Spirit Week" activities preceding Homecoming weekend helped boost student pride for their school— and within themselves.

Also, Van Horn didn't have a drama club. "There hadn't been a student production in 10 or 15 years," Layden says. But with their new teachers' encouragement, students formed a group called Van Horn Stages, rehearsed, built sets, sold tickets and performed the play "Barefoot in the Park" and the musical "You're A Good Man, Charlie Brown" for delighted audiences.

Student Council President Anthony Mondaine, a member of Pastor Clarence Newton's nearby Greater New Home Baptist Church, was asked by *The Examiner* for his thoughts about the "new" Van Horn. "I don't want to bash the Kansas City School District," Mondaine said, "but Independence has really given us Christmas. They have given us opportunities we didn't even know we had."

At the end of Van Horn's first year as an integral part of the Independence School District, the number of college-bound students nearly tripled that of the previous year—Mondaine was one of them. Says Layden: "Being able to go into that school and prove that a semi-urban high school can be changed for the better—without being a charter school or private school—and that the public school model can work and help kids respond in positive ways is enormously gratifying, better than I ever imagined it could be."

It was a clean break from the Kansas City School District. Virtually all teachers and principals at the annexed schools were newly hired and all passionately committed to "making a difference," says Dr. R.D. Mallams, the new principal at North Rock Creek/Korte Elementary School. (As it turned out, most Kansas City teachers didn't apply for positions, in order to protect their pensions and benefits.)

The Independence School District made special efforts to hire new teachers "dedicated to developing relationships with kids and ensuring that those kids develop knowledge that prepares them for life after high school," notes Dr. Netzer, himself hired in March 2008 for his compassionate administrative expertise.

"Over the course of that first year after school boundary change," Hinson says, "we received favorable commentary from many parents involved at all the annexed schools who believe the 'whole-student' approach we offer makes a very productive difference in their children's lives." That approach includes the district's after-school programs conducted by social workers to help "at-risk" students and families.

Hinson cites a local meeting he attended a few years earlier where discussion focused on neighborhood reform, high crime and student dropout rates. "A minister stood up and said, 'This occurs because people don't have any hope; they don't have hope for a better way of life for their children. They don't have hope that they can improve their situation.'

"I equated that to what people were facing in Western Independence and Sugar Creek at the time. Many people believed their kids and their neighborhoods didn't have any hope because of the educational situation they were mired in. They found a solution in school boundary change, and our district embraced them. When I looked at data showing that there were kids in the Kansas City School District who were being 'lost' at an early age, and that many of them were destined to live a life of poverty, in many cases a life of crime, I thought, 'How could our district not be willing to say, 'We can take care of you as well.'"

Photo courtesy of *The Examiner*.

Photo courtesy of *The Examiner*.

Van Horn High School alum and retired Major League Baseball pitching ace Rick Sutcliffe returned to Independence in April 2009 to help celebrate community rebirth after the Independence School District annexation occurred. Hundreds of local residents had renovated R. J. Roper Stadium where he played baseball as a kid. Misty-eyed, Sutcliffe told everybody the community had earned "a second chance."

Thirty-four-year-old Jeff Anger (pronounced AN-jer) is the new principal at Fairmount Elementary School. An Independence native whose mother is a teacher, he hired 30 new teachers and staff and participated in the Extreme School Makeover before moving into his office and assuming responsibility for 360 students.

Fairmount, a beautiful brick structure built in 1928, is a landmark in one of the area's most impoverished neighborhoods. Students in subsidized free and reduced-cost lunch programs there comprise the district's highest participation rate. Yet that is not evident as you walk through the school's newly painted classrooms and hallways (Anger calls the vanilla color "Fairmount Cream"), see its 30 new computers and watch kids play on colorful new playground equipment.

"One of the things I believe is so positive and powerful about this changeover is that it helps people feel like they have an identity associated with their schools and are part of a progressive community," Anger says. "When I was a kid in elementary school, I lived three blocks from the border between the Independence and Kansas City School Districts. Crossing that border just felt like a different world. When you're a kid you wonder, 'If this is all Independence, why isn't this neighborhood part of our school district?' I had friends who lived on the other side but they didn't go to the Kansas City School District schools there—they went to parochial schools.

"A couple of years ago, before all this happened, I was very skeptical that it could be pulled off. This type of change for a community, annexing seven schools and their territory in the modern political age we live in, would be pretty miraculous, if not seemingly impossible. It took a *lot* of people really believing in the same idea. I remember being amazed when the votes came in and so many people in Kansas City were supportive. But all those people on both sides of the boundary believed this would be good for their kids.

"Is this going to be an overnight miracle, where all of a sudden we're in a land filled with milk and honey? No. It's not going to happen overnight. But as we progress and as more families realize they really have a vested interest in this community school, I believe the school will improve, the kids will improve and their families' lives will improve."

Anger explains one reason for his optimism: "When I was hiring teachers and staff, the first trait I looked for was empathy. I searched for people who could look at a kid and recognize what they were going through. I wanted them to truly love kids, to have a passion for helping each and every individual kid achieve all that they can.

"To me, empathy is the key to so much, because if you're empathetic and you love that kid, and you love that classroom, you will do all you can to help them. If you need to learn a different skill, you're going to *want* to learn that skill. So I was looking for empathetic people who are also flexible and passionate teachers. Interviewing is a very inexact science, so I feel very blessed. I feel like I won the lottery, with every staff member we have!

"When we started here, almost none of my staff knew each other. Now deep bonds have been formed. When you think about all that has happened in the lives of our staff members, our kids and their families—who are now *our* families—it's truly remarkable. We are helping our community grow in a positive way. It is definitely a positive to have more interaction between Fairmount Elementary school and our community."

Hinson agrees. "I believe community interaction is a hallmark within the Independence School District that has distinguished our Board of Education, the administration, faculty and staff for many years. There is no question that this quality has expanded powerfully since the school boundary change.

"We find a yearning in this community and strong desires among people to sustain and grow the momentum they established during the annexation drive and Extreme School Makeover. I believe this is based partly on hope, partly on pride and rooted in goals to make our neighborhoods better places to live, work and go to school.

"That may sound kind of corny, but as you look around our community you can see the pervasive sense of accomplishment people feel arising from school boundary change and the fact they united in common cause to make it happen. These are proud people. We feel the same way.

"One of our commitments is to nurture this pride and achievement, help fuel the momentum and take enlightened steps to support it as best we can. You might say we are strengthening our partnerships with people and organizations in Sugar Creek and throughout our city. It is an inspiring mission, filled with purpose."

At Hinson's invitation, Van Horn alum and retired Major League Baseball pitching ace Rick Sutcliffe—"The Red Baron"—returned to his alma mater in April 2009 for the first time in decades to see its many improvements. *The Examiner* reported, "As he walked through the halls, visited the new refurbished gymnasium and found his old locker in the boys' locker room, he got misty eyed and said 'I've got goose bumps. Man, I'm glad I came back here.'"

The former Falcons all-star pitched a wiffle ball game, signed autographs, visited students, then joined Hinson and Missouri State Representative Ray Salva for a trip to nearby Roper Stadium, the public park where he'd learned to throw as a kid. It was exactly as he remembered … except better.

Hundreds of Independence and Sugar Creek residents had fixed up the park and its field in a volunteer "Mini-Makeover" on March 22 coordinated by the Independence School District to preserve the civic initiative begun with the Extreme School Makeover. Sutcliff called it "amazing! This really gives you a lift." Mobbed by kids, he told them that baseball scouts recruiting him years earlier were just as interested in his grade point average as his fastball.

On "Rick Sutcliffe Day" hosted by the Independence School District for its famous native son a few weeks later, Sutcliffe reaffirmed that their victorious fight to control their educational destiny was indeed extraordinary. The previous year, he'd battled, and beaten, colon cancer, earning what he called "a second chance." He told people that they, too, had fought a tough battle to earn a second chance for their community. He promised to come back often.

Today, the Independence School District is helping students discover new educational opportunities and attracting new families to the district's annexed neighborhoods. Stability and growth are slowly returning to Western Independence and Sugar Creek. Civic leaders are leveraging the annexation's positive impact.

"Boosting economic development in Western Independence is number one on our action plan list," declares Rick Hemmingsen, CEO of the Independence Chamber of Commerce, which has prioritized improvements in infrastructure, housing, public safety and business development for the annexed school area.

Already, the City of Independence has launched infrastructure improvements in the Englewood, Maywood and Fairmount neighborhoods, including sidewalks, roads and bridges. First District City Councilwoman Marcie Gragg has been extensively involved with The Great Northwest Independence Neighborhood Initiative, a project supported by City Hall. It divided Western Independence into neighborhood groups whose residents are developing "front porch" agendas to address key areas of concern: quality of life, public works and utilities, safety, and health.

Independence Mayor Don Reimal says those agendas will be incorporated into a strategic neighborhood improvement plan that the city will execute. Fourth District Councilman Jim Page, a former Independence police officer, is promoting commercial development in Western Independence with two new tax-supported business initiatives recently introduced by the Independence Council for Economic Development.

Even in the slow economy, rehabbing and home renovations are rebounding in Western Independence thanks, in part, to the Missouri 353 tax abatement program recently launched there, offering tax relief to owners who make property improvements. In Sugar Creek, a new 244,000-square-foot shopping plaza called "SugarLand" and anchored by a major grocery store, is being built. Matt Mallinson, school leader for the ESM at Sugar Creek Elementary School and recent appointee to the Independence School District Board of Education, is moving his pharmacy there from across the street.

In March 2009 the Independence Council for Economic Development commissioned a feasibility study for establishing a dynamic arts and entertainment district in the historic Englewood Station area where the Englewood Theatre stands. It is supported by the City of Independence, the Englewood Business Association and the Truman Heartland Foundation.

"These and other activities are positive signs that the school boundary change is generating benefits for our community in more ways than one," says Pastor Spradling. With Jim Reynolds of the nonprofit North-West Communities Development Corporation, Spradling is spearheading new home construction and renovation of others for buyers receiving low-cost mortgages along the Independence-Sugar Creek border.

In April 2009 Hinson announced that the school district will be lead partner in the Independence Regional Ennovation Center, a business incubator and education facility which opened in January 2010 on the site of a former hospital. The district reserved 254,000 square feet of renovated space for start-up businesses, bio-technology labs, district programs and support services.

Because the Ennovation Center is funded by tax-increment financing payments and rental income, no money from the school district's budget is being used for the project, whose co-partners are the City of Independence, CEAH Realtors and the Independence Council for Economic Development.

Hinson calls the Ennovation Center a "win-win. We are extremely enthusiastic about this synergy between our district, the city and private sector investors to support business progress and inventive new programs. We are excited for our district and community. This will help create jobs, retain jobs and showcase young entrepreneurs."

———————————

On the weekend of July 18, 2009, Independence and Sugar Creek citizens again showed their enthusiasm for partnering with the Independence School District and their neighborhood schools. More than 1,000 volunteers joined in "Project Shine" to spruce up five schools, including three acquired in the annexation. Once more, citizens showed up with shovels, ladders, paint, flowers and positive attitudes.

"None of those schools showed poor conditions," notes Worth Smith, who helped organize the event. "But people in the community wanted to pick up where the Extreme School Makeover left off and sustain its momentum, so they rallied support and volunteered. It was a great day and a wonderful 'refresher.' We hope Project Shine will be an annual event."

The Extreme School Makeover and Project Shine have taught the Independence School District many lessons, says Hinson: "Since the school boundary change occurred and we welcomed more than 2,600 new students to the annexed school properties, our school district has learned a great deal. We've learned that people truly do care about public education and related service programs that make positive differences in their lives, and will fight for it.

"We also learned that our community and our patrons rely on our school district for more than educational opportunity and supportive family services. Our community relies on the Independence School District for civic leadership.

"In this regard, we believe that collaborating with our community creates great energy and enthusiasm for what we stand for. We believe it engages parents to become more involved with their children's schools. We believe it maximizes the potential for helping students with positive role modeling, which can help our children succeed.

"When people in Western Independence and Sugar Creek asked us to help improve education and neighborhood quality of life with school boundary change, we assumed an enormous responsibility," Hinson says. "Yet we also discovered great occasions and enthusiasm for advancing local progress.

"Does this reflect well on the Independence School District? I believe it does. But I believe it more importantly reflects on the people who live and work here who demonstrated their faith, hope and desires and are relying on education to truly build a better future," he says.

"When an organization, a group of people or even one person has achieved a goal of this magnitude—an awakening, a redemption or whatever you may wish to call it, and assumes responsibility for it—there is no going back to the way things used to be. We can only move forward with an enlightened sense of purpose, commitment and achievement."

———————

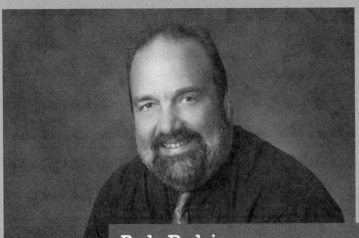

Bob Robinson
Director of Facilities, Independence School District

Bob Robinson focused on diverse building maintenance and upgrade issues during the Independence School District annexation initiative, starting with his hands-on management to ensure safe and effective operations at six schools annexed from the Kansas City School District in November 2007.

His responsibilities were hampered by the Kansas City School District's initial refusals to allow Robinson and his staff to conduct thorough inspections of the annexed facilities. His extended access to heating and air conditioning systems, elevators, plumbing, electrical, security and other systems—even playgrounds and landscaping—was delayed for months as arbitration to settle disputes between the two school districts and legal actions ensued.

Robinson worried that the annexed schools would not be in suitable operating condition for students arriving on opening day in August 2008. At a court hearing on July 7, 2008, his testimony helped convince a judge to grant the Independence School District immediate access to the properties. "I had never testified in court before," says Robinson. He found most of the annexed schools "in extremely bad shape" when he finally got in to inspect them, he says.

Robinson's facilities planning for the Extreme School Makeover to help improve school conditions was crucial. He helped recruit expert craftsmen from local labor unions as volunteer workers, met with volunteer school team leaders to coordinate renovation activities and developed action plans for volunteer teams. He also scrounged donations of literally tons of supplies for the hugely successful Extreme School Makeover that occurred July 26-27, 2008.

An Independence resident employed by the Independence School District for nearly 20 years, Robinson had seen annexation fever grow across the region over the previous 18 months. "I attended almost all of the town hall meetings where people discussed annexation," he says, "because I thought that if we could make Western Independence and Sugar Creek schools better for local families and kids, the whole community would be better.

"It was amazing to see people pull together to vote for the school boundary change and help make all this happen," Robinson says. As a result: "I foresee new families moving in and this being good for our community."

1. Paul Ciotti's article "Money and School Performance: Lessons from the Kansas City Desegregation Experiment" was published on March 16, 1998, by the Cato Institute, a nonprofit policy research foundation headquartered in Washington, D.C. Ciotti lives in Los Angeles, California and writes about education.

2. Members of "The 11th Senatorial District Task Force for the Improvement of Education in Western Independence and Sugar Creek" in 2004 included Ken McClain, an attorney in Independence; Mayor of Independence Ron Stewart; Don Reimal, the 1st District Councilman for the city of Independence; Dennis Waits, an attorney in Independence and 3rd District representative in the Jackson County legislature; Paul Wrabec, a businessman in Sugar Creek; Terry Young, 49th District representative in the Missouri House; Dr. Rowena Ferguson, president of Christian Bible College and Seminary; and Don Ross, a retired Independence School District elementary school principal living in Western Independence.

3. In research conducted in 2006 and 2007, the Independence School District could not identify any U.S. public school annexation of the size and scope of that being considered in Western Independence and Sugar Creek and, to the district's knowledge, no similar annexation of such size and scope has occurred.

4. Based in Jefferson City, the Missouri Ethics Commission monitors citizens, public officials and lobbyists participating in elections. It also enforces campaign finance, personal financial disclosure and conflict of interest laws.

5. The Kansas City School District allowed representatives of the Independence School District to enter the annexed schools on several occasions for short periods of time between December 2007 and June 2008. However, that access was very limited and did not allow for inspection of the premises' conditions or inventories. The Independence School District was allowed full access to the annexed school buildings by the Kansas City School District on the afternoon of July 7, 2009, when Judge Jack Grate ruled the Independence School District would suffer "immediate and irreparable harm" if transfer of the annexed schools was delayed any longer. His ruling gave the Independence School District unlimited access to all of the annexed school buildings and

their contents. Until that ruling, Independence School District officials could not conduct inspections to determine the buildings' conditions.

6. The Kansas City School District's initial request to receive $157.29 million from the Independence School District to settle financial disputes between the two school districts regarding the annexation was modified during the first arbitration hearing on April 24, 2008. There, an attorney for the Kansas City School District told the arbitration panel that an error had been made when the apportionment proposal for the Kansas City School District was being prepared for submission to the panel on April 22. The Kansas City School District's annexation settlement request was changed from $157.29 million to approximately $90 million during that first arbitration hearing.

7. The School District of Kansas City Building Corporation is a nonprofit corporation that owned the seven annexed schools in Western Independence and Sugar Creek and leased them to the Kansas City School District prior to the school boundary change vote of November 2007. It is an entity separate from the Kansas City School District, with its own board of directors. It was formed in 1984 to provide for acquisition, construction, improvement, repair and remodeling of public school sites within the Kansas City School District. This school property ownership issue became a focus of the arbitration proceedings between the Kansas City and Independence School Districts that occurred in mid-2008. It later became the focus of an application for a temporary restraining order that the School District of Kansas City Building Corporation filed against the Independence School District in June 2008 to delay the Independence School District's possession of the annexed school buildings. The annexed school property ownership issue was resolved on August 7, 2008, when the Independence School District paid approximately $12.8 million to receive titles for the seven annexed schools and one additional building.

8. Roger Dorson and Tom Quinn are employed by the Missouri Department of Elementary and Secondary Education (DESE). Official legal opinions for DESE are issued by its Office of General Counsel.

9. Ibid; see second Chapter Eleven endnote above.

10. The Independence School District Citizens Advisory & Transition Committee was created in early 2008 by Dr. Jim Hinson. It combined members of two committees that Hinson had formed: a Citizens Advisory Committee founded in 2004 (30 members), and a Transition Committee created immediately after the school boundary change vote occurred in November 2007 (50 members). The Citizens Advisory & Transition Committee meets routinely with Hinson and other Independence School District administrators to discuss educational and community issues.

11. The Independence School District incorporates early childhood programs, before-and-after school programs, wellness education, nutritional services and family support services into each of the district's neighborhood schools. A crowd of more than 1,300 parents and community members volunteer regularly to assist with many school, family and community activities. The Independence School District also offers after-school programs conducted by social workers to help "at-risk" students and families.

Acknowledgments

Without the involvement and resources of many people and organizations, this book would not have been possible. The Independence School District would like to thank deeply each and every person who participated in this project for generous contributions of their time for interviews and providing resource materials essential for compiling information useful in developing the manuscript. We extend our sincere thanks and appreciation to:

- Jeff Dunlap of St. Louis, Missouri, who compiled the research, conducted all the interviews and wrote this book on behalf of the Independence School District, Board of Education and Dr. Jim Hinson.

- Lori Worth Smith, Executive Director for the School District of Independence Foundation and President of Vibe Marketing Group in Independence, who rendered extensive creative advice and counsel for the project.

- Rick Skwiot of Key West, Florida, who provided editorial counsel.

- The Harry S. Truman Library and Museum in Independence for access to and use of archival information about the early life of late President Harry S. Truman when he was a student in the Independence School District, and as a retired citizen.

- *The Examiner* daily newspaper and its Internet-based archival news library, NewsBank, Inc. of Naples, Florida, for online access to and use of historic news articles and information originally published in *The Examiner* and archived by NewsBank.

- Education writer Paul Ciotti for the fair use citations from his article "Lessons from the Kansas City Desegregation Experiment," published by The Cato Institute, a non-profit public policy research foundation headquartered in Washington, D.C.

- *TIME* magazine and *The New York Times* for the fair use citations which appear in this book as noted herein and excerpted from articles that were originally published by those news organizations.

- The Independence Chamber of Commerce for the resources and facilities that the Chamber made available to the Independence School District when conducting interviews for this project.

- Thank you Truman Heartland Community Foundation for your contribution to the book project.

Finally, we again thank the students, faculty, staff, friends and patrons of the Independence School District, residents of Independence and Sugar Creek, Missouri, and the municipal governments of Independence and Sugar Creek, for their support during the momentous school annexation process that is the focus of this manuscript.

Maywood Baptist Church was one of many organizations in Independence and the neighboring city of Sugar Creek that encouraged people to participate in a public forum on February 9, 2006, to discuss the potentials of school boundary change. As a result, that forum was attended by a capacity crowd of local citizens who voiced their concerns.

A WORD FROM OUR PASTOR

Thank You Gary and Debbie

On behalf of the Maywood Church family, I want to express our appreciation to Gary and Debbie for thirteen years of ministry among us. We all can recall the times when Gary wrote a song and sang it for the first time at Maywood. The use of instruments and the projection system were gifts that Gary brought to Maywood. Visitors to our congregation remark about how effectively we use audio-visuals in our worship services. Again, this is the impact that Gary has made on Maywood. Under Gary's leadership we have an excellent sound system that should serve us for many more years.

I think Gary's greatest contribution is his emphasis on worship. Worship to Gary is far more than singing songs before a sermon. Corporate worship is our expression to God who is worthy of our devotion. Gary has helped us express our worship to God in ways that touch deep places in our lives. We thank God for leading Gary to help us pursue Him in worship.

Debbie has wonderfully served our congregation as an occasional director of the choir, a valued Sunday School teacher and Journey Group leader. Debbie has impacted numerous women in our congregation with her Christ-centered life.

On behalf of the congregation, I express our prayers for God's very best in Gary's new song-writing career. We pray that God will profoundly bless and direct Gary for the sake of the entire body of Christ. What Gary shared with us has the potential of being expanded far beyond our own congregation. Again, thanks and may God bless you richly Gary and Debbie.

School Meeting - Tuesday, July 31 at 7:00pm

For Northwest Independence the long-awaited time has come. Our community is ready to seek a change in the school system that serves our children and teens. Numerous individuals and circumstances make the next few months crucial in the process that will take seven current KCMO schools and place them in the Independence School District.

Maywood Baptist will host a community meeting on this subject on Tuesday, July 31. The meeting will begin at 7:00 pm in our auditorium. Dr. Jim Hinson, Superintendent of the Independence School System, will be present to present a vision of what will happen in the seven schools. Mr. Steve Mauer, an attorney and Chairman of the Independence Chamber of Commerce Board, will present a legal picture of what must happen for the change to take place. Senator Victor Callahan, Representative Ray Salva, Mayor Stan Salva, and Councilperson Marcie Gragg will be present to share the process that citizens must take to insure a victory for this cause. Please note, Mayor Don Reimal has played a significant and important role in this process. He will be out of town on the 31st.

Who needs to be present at this meeting? Church members should be informed so we can pray and add assistance where possible. Parents of students in the Kansas City school system should also be present. I hope to see a large number of Maywood people in our auditorium this Tuesday night at 7:00 pm.

-Bob Spradling

Thanks!
Sunday School Children's Division

Building a Strong Foundation of Faith in the Lives of our Children

Week by week these faithful leaders are creatively teaching the children how God has been at work in our world and how He continues to be at work in our lives.

Grades 1 and 2
Lona Smith, director, Susan Reed and Ray Martin

Grades 3 and 4
Jo Beebe and Pam Deason, co-directors,
Gayle Davidson, Ruby Adams, Al Peters, Phil Hickman

Grades 5 and 6
Tim Driller, Jr. and Sherry Carroll co-directors
Larry Ryner, Tracy Martin, Monica Carter

Division Director - Toni Spradling

"I thank my God every time I remember you. In all my prayers for all of you, I always pray with joy because of your partnership in the gospel..." Philippians 1:3-5a

To help get out the vote for school annexation, Missouri State Senator Victor Callahan produced pro-annexation flyers, posters and letters that appealed to different educational, political and cultural interests of voters living in both the Independence and Kansas City School Districts.

LET'S GIVE OUR KIDS A CHANCE!

CAMPAIGN RALLY

October 2, 2007

6:30 - 8:00 pm

Roper Stadium
131 S. Carlisle Sugar Creek

Carlisle is two blocks West of Sterling on 24 Hwy. Turn North at the Taco Bell.
(Follow the signs on Sterling)

WE NEED YOUR HELP

The Campaign for quality education for the children of Independence and Sugar Creek has begun! Bring your friends and family to this important event.

Financial Support
Make checks payable to:

KIDS ARE OUR FUTURE
11211 WINNER RD.
INDEPENDENCE, MO 64052

This is the first of many press releases distributed by the Independence School District to inform media of delays that the district encountered during arbitration proceedings to resolve financial issues of the school annexation. Arbitration had commenced on April 24, 2008, but a decision was not reached until late June, more than two months later.

BOARD OF ARBITRATION CALLS ON DISTRICTS TO REACH AGREEMENT

For more information:
Dr. Jim Hinson
Superintendent of Schools
Independence, Missouri Public School District
816-521-5300, Ext. 10054

FOR IMMEDIATE RELEASE – April 24, 2008

Independence, MO –

The Missouri State Board of Education-appointed Board of Arbitration did not reach a decision today during the hearing held at Union Station concerning the annexation of seven schools from the Kansas City, Missouri School District to the Independence School District. The board did, however, shift responsibility to the superintendents of both districts by requesting the superintendents work one-on-one to reach a final decision within the next week. The board requested the superintendents return a signed agreement by April 30 to execute the transition. If a mutual plan is not presented jointly by Independence Superintendent, Dr. Jim Hinson and Kansas City Interim Superintendent, Dr. John Martin, the Board of Arbitration will proceed with their review process and render a final decision.

Dr. Jim Hinson is approaching his meetings with Dr. Martin with the intent of expediting the annexation swiftly, while ensuring the best interests of the students and families involved. "It is important that we do what is right by the children in our new schools and the families in Independence and Sugar Creek," states Hinson.

KMBC-TV Channel 9, an ABC Television Network affiliate in Kansas City that serves the region, covered the school boundary change issue and related legal battles between the Independence and Kansas City School Districts starting in 2006, as did other Missouri media. In editorials, KMBC-TV voiced its support for the Independence School District's annexation of seven schools managed by the Kansas City School District, and so did regional newspapers including *Kansas City Star* and *The Examiner*.

KMBC-TV EDITORIAL

Air: 7/19/08, 7/20/08, 7/21/08

IT IS AN EMBARRASSMENT AND A WASTE OF TAX DOLLARS. THE KANSAS CITY SCHOOL DISTRICT CONTINUES TO SPEND ENTIRELY TOO MUCH OF ITS ENERGY AND MONEY RESISTING THE TRANSFER OF SEVEN SCHOOL BUILDINGS TO THE INDEPENDENCE SCHOOL DISTRICT.

VOTERS OVERWHELMINGLY APPROVED DISTRICT BOUNDARY CHANGES LAST NOVEMBER. LAST MONTH, ARBITRATORS SET A PRICE FOR THE BUILDINGS. THE DECISION IS NOW IN THE HANDS OF A JACKSON COUNTY JUDGE.

LIKE SO MANY OF OUR VIEWERS, WE QUESTION WHY THE KANSAS CITY SCHOOL DISTRICT CONTINUES THIS FIGHT. IS IT ABOUT THE CHILDREN? NOT HARDLY. IT'S ABOUT MONEY. MONEY THAT COULD HAVE AND SHOULD HAVE BEEN SPENT, NOT ON LAWYERS, BUT ON THE EDUCATION OF THE DISTRICT'S CHILDREN.

IF THE KANSAS CITY SCHOOL BOARD FOCUSED THIS KIND OF ATTENTION ON STUDENT ACHIEVEMENT, TEST SCORES MIGHT BE HIGHER AND GRADUATION RATES INCREASED. FULL ACCREDITATION COULD BE MORE THAN JUST A DISTANT HOPE.

Delivered by:
Wayne Godsey
President & General Manager

Editorials run: Saturday morning after First News Weekend Edition (8:56 am)
Saturday evening after the 6:00 pm News (6:56 pm)
Sunday morning after First News Weekend Edition (8:56 am)
Sunday evening after the 5:30 pm News (5:57 pm)
Sunday evening after the 10:00 pm News (10:56 pm)
Monday morning preceding "Good Morning America" (6:56 am)

Editorial reprint courtesy of KMBC-TV.

In letters to Independence School District patrons and community leaders, Superintendent Dr. Jim Hinson announced plans for an all-volunteer "Extreme School Makeover" that would occur the weekend of July 26-27, 2008. The goal was to renovate the annexed school buildings before schools opened in August, and to celebrate community pride.

Dr. Jim Hinson, Superintendent
3225 South Noland Road
Independence, Missouri 64055
(816) 521-5300   Fax (816) 521-2999

Dear Patrons,

This is an exciting time to be a part of the Independence School District. While we have faced challenges during this process of transitioning our new schools in western Independence and Sugar Creek into the district, we are thrilled to welcome these students and their families. In an effort to ready these schools and greet the children, parents, faculty and staff of these schools with a new beginning, we are coordinating Extreme School Makeover July 26 and 27. This makeover weekend will mobilize hundreds of great people like you to refresh and revitalize our new buildings. We hope you will join us to help make a difference for the nearly 2500 kids attending these schools.

We've had a phenomenal response from individuals, organized groups and businesses who want to be a part of Extreme School Makeover, but more help is needed. Some of these facilities are in dire need of attention as a result of years of neglect. Volunteers will team together to perform various clean up and maintenance tasks such as, painting, window washing, light repairs and landscaping. Although we will be working hard, we are hoping to make this event both meaningful and enjoyable for the volunteers. Any time commitment you can make will truly make an impact. We know it will be awe-inspiring for everyone to see our community come together for this worthwhile cause.

In addition to volunteers, donations of landscaping items, paint, building supplies and materials, or cash donations to purchase these items, would be much appreciated. Please contact us if you and/or your company are willing to be a donor or a major sponsor of this event.

To sign up as a volunteer, be a sponsor or get more info, please visit www.OurNewSchools.com. You may also call our Extreme School Makeover information line at 816-521-5502 or email extremeinfo@indep.k12.mo.us.

Thank you for your interest in helping the Independence School District. It's caring people like you who will make a difference in our new schools and our community. You will be making these buildings welcoming and inspiring for students, families, faculty and staff members to enter this fall. We hope you will find the experience personally rewarding as well.

Sincerely,

Dr. Jim Hinson
Superintendent

EXTREME
SCHOOL MAKEOVER
Get Involved.
★   ★   ★   ★   ★

Led by its founder Lori Worth Smith, Vibe Marketing Group created many promotional materials to recruit volunteers for the Extreme School Makeover that occurred in July 2008. Posters, brochures and flyers distributed to local businesses, civic organizations, churches and fraternal groups attracted thousands of volunteers.

Get Involved.

Lifting Hammers. Lifting Spirits.

Call the Extreme School Makeover hotline at 816-521-5502 or extremeinfo@indep.k12.mo.us

Welcome our new schools in western Independence and Sugar Creek by becoming a part of **Extreme School Makeover**. The Independence School District is leading this effort to refresh and update our new schools in time for students returning this fall as part of the Independence School District family.

Extreme School Makeover event dates are set for July 26/27.*
We Need: Hands-On Volunteers • Supplies • Corporate Sponsors**

Monetary Donations: Make checks payable to: The School District of Independence Foundation, Inc. and mail to Extreme School Makeover, 3225 S. Noland Rd., Independence, MO 64055

*Event dates are tentative and subject to change.
**Volunteers must be 16 years of age or older

Independence
SCHOOL DISTRICT
Inspiring Greatness

In addition to volunteers, the Extreme School Makeover required tons of tools and materials to be successful. These included items shown on this list, plus bulldozers, back-hoes, dump trucks, cement mix, garbage bins, chain saws, wood chippers, picks, shovels, rakes, plants, mulch, landscape supplies, and tall ladders.

Makeover Supply List

If you have items to donate or lend to the event, they may be dropped off at the Independence School District Central Office at 3225 S. Noland Rd. Questions? Call Extreme School Makeover hotline at **816-521-5502**

Items to Donate	Quantity Needed	Items to Donate and/or Lend to the Event	Quantity Needed
Heavy Work Gloves	500	Leaf Rakes	25
Regular Work Gloves	500	Garden Rakes	25
Safety Glasses	200	Wheel Barrows	25
Ear Plugs	200	Sharp Shooter Shovels	50
First Aid Kits	6	Round Point Shovels	50
Hand Shears	25	Painting Tarps	200
Trash Bags - 55 gallon - Extra Heavy Duty	250 boxes	Step Ladders	50
Pairs of Landscaping Gloves	100	Ladders	25
Paint Brushes	500	Lawn Sprinklers	75
Paint Rollers	400	50 Foot Garden Hoses	300
Paint Roller Handles	300	50 Foot Soaker Hoses	100
Paint Thinner	25	Red Landscape Mulch	
Hand Cleaner	50	Dirt	
Paint Scrapers	100	Box Fans	200
Rags—Box O Rags	50 boxes	Large Fans	30
Sponges	200	Floor Vacuums	20
Glass Cleaner	50	Buckets	50
Squeegees—10"	100	Brooms	50
Utility Knives	100	Mops	50
Utility Knife—Flat Blades for Refills	Box of 100	Dust Pans	50
Ceiling Tile, 2x4, drop-in	100 cases	Megaphones	6
Red Curb Paint 5 gallons per site	30 gal		
Hats for Painters	1000		
Latex Paint (Pittsburg #2511 Creamy White)	650 Gallons		
Pop	2,500 to 3,000		
Bottled Water	120 Cases		

*The Independence School District is not responsible for loss or damage of borrowed items.

Advance promotion of the Extreme School Makeover to recruit volunteer workers and donations of supplies included billboards, which were strategically placed along major highways in Western Independence, Sugar Creek and other high-profile locations in the region.

The Independence School District's outreach to potential sponsors for the Extreme School Makeover helped raise more than $116,000 in cash and $432,000 in supplies, services and media co-sponsorships to ensure a successful event.

CORPORATE SPONSORSHIP PACKAGES

Sign up today for this very limited unique opportunity to support the Independence community and promote your business!
Extreme School Makeover Weekend
Scheduled for July 26 & 27*
*Dates subject to change

Media	Platinum $45,000	Gold $30,000	Silver $22,000	Bronze $14,500	Varsity $5,500	Jr. Varsity $1200	Community $500
KMBC -TV 9 News Shows (Platinum/Gold include Extreme Home Makeover Program)	65 thirty-second commercials; 10 five-second news billboards mentions; online video featured sponsor	38 thirty-second commercials; 5 five-second news billboard mentions	35 thirty-second commercials	26 thirty-second commercials	N/A	N/A	N/A
KUDL 98.1, WDAF 106.5, KMBZ 980	2-week campaign on WDAF, KUDL, KMBZ - 175 spots/mentions; 1 remote (KUDL or WDAF); 3 email blasts; Web display ads	2-week campaign on KUDL & KMBZ - 100 spots/mentions; 1 Remote (KUDL); 3 email blasts; Web display ads	1-week campaign on WDAF & KUDL - 84 spots/mentions; 1 Remote (KUDL or WDAF); 1 email blast; shared Web display ads	1-week campaign on 1 station (KUDL WDAF or KMBZ) - 26 spots/mentions; 1 email blast; shared Web display ads	3 email blasts; shared Web display ads	N/A	N/A
Examiner - 2 Special Sections	2 full-page color ads	2 half-page color ads	1 half-page color & 1 quarter-page color ad	2 quarter-page color ads	2 eighth-page color ads	Business Listing	N/A
The KC Star (Mon-Sat "A" or Local Section; ads to include ESM content)	1 half-page b/w ad	1 quarter-page b/w ad	1 eighth-page b/w ad	N/A	N/A	N/A	N/A
Independence Chamber of Commerce (ISD Insert in Newsletter)	Platinum Sponsor Placement	Gold Sponsor Placement	Silver Sponsor Placement	Business Card Ad	Logo Business Listing	Business Listing	N/A
Interactive Website Linked Logo/Listing (*listing only)	KMBC.com, KUDL.com, 1065THEWOLF.com, KMBZ.com, Examiner.net, indep.k12.mo.us	KMBC.com, KUDL.com, 1065THEWOLF.com, KMBZ.com, Examiner.net, indep.k12.mo.us	KMBC.com, KUDL.com, 1065THEWOLF.com, KMBZ.com, Examiner.net, indep.k12.mo.us	KMBC.com indep.k12.mo.us	KMBC.com* indep.k12.mo.us	indep.k12.mo.us*	indep.k12.mo.us*
Event T-shirt	Company Logo	Company Logo	Company Logo	N/A	N/A	N/A	N/A
Event Signage	Platinum Placement/Logo	Gold Placement/Logo	Silver Placement/Logo	Bronze Placement/Logo	Bold Business Listing	Business Listing	Business Listing

EXTREME SCHOOL MAKEOVER - MAKE IT HAPPEN!   Sponsorship Level: _____

Company Name: _____   Contact Name: _____

Phone: _____   Alt. Phone: _____   Email: _____

Mailing Address: _____

Do you have an employee group or individuals interested in volunteering at the event? If so, how many? _____

Is your company interested in donating supplies for the event? _____ What type of supplies can you donate? (Please list items and quantity.) _____

By signing and dating below, I agree to sponsor Extreme School Makeover at the level noted above.

Signature: _____   Date: __/__/__ Title: _____

Please make checks payable to *The School District of Independence Foundation, Inc.* and mail to Extreme School Makeover, 3225 S. Noland Rd, Independence, MO 64055. For further information, contact the Independence School District's Extreme School Makeover Office at 816-521-5502 or extremeinfo@indep.k12.mo.us

Category exclusivity for sponsors at Platinum, Gold and Silver levels.
A portion of sponsorship investment may be tax deductible; consult your tax advisor for eligibility.

Independence
SCHOOL DISTRICT
Inspiring Greatness

The Independence Chamber of Commerce supported the school boundary change initiative and the Extreme School Makeover by keeping its stakeholders informed of Independence School District activities. Several Chamber board members served as crucial leaders in the annexation process.

Independence *Chamber News*

Volume 37, No.   This issue is sponsored by: Sheraton Kansas City Sports Complex   June 2008

INSIDE THIS ISSUE

2 NEW MEMBERS

3 CHAMBER EVENTS & RIBBON CUTTINGS

4 BUSINESS BRIEFS

5 FROM OUR SPONSOR
SHERATON KANSAS CITY SPORTS COMPLEX

8 CALENDAR OF EVENTS

Independence Chamber of Commerce

THE INDEPENDENCE CHAMBER NEWSLETTER IS PRINTED BY:

CORPORATE **CopyPrint** INC.

EXTREME SCHOOL MAKEOVER
Get Involved.

(Submitted by the Independence School District)

As you may know, the Independence School District is growing. As a result of the recent voter-approved change in boundaries in western Independence and Sugar Creek, approximately 2500 new students and their school buildings will become a part of the district for the 2008-2009 academic year. With this transition, the Independence School District is coordinating an Extreme School Makeover weekend July 26th and 27th to refresh and revitalize the school buildings for students, families, faculty and staff returning this fall as part of the Independence School District family.

Currently, the buildings are in various states of disrepair. Issues range from holes in walls and ceilings to missing floor tiles to weed-infested and debris-filled playgrounds to larger HVAC, electrical and structural problems. While Extreme School Makeover will not resolve all issues with these buildings, it will go a long way in establishing a foundation for change and creating welcoming, enriching learning environments for the district's new students.

The district is encouraging Independence businesses to rally behind this initiative with volunteers and sponsorships. This is a unique opportunity to show your pride in Independence and make a tangible, positive impact in the lives of our youth and community as a whole. This is an exciting time and your chance to get involved and help build unity in Independence!

Sponsorships, volunteers and supplies are needed to make Extreme School Makeover a success. The district is offering multiple sponsorship levels which include media exposure for participating businesses. Businesses may elect to participate by sending volunteer teams to assist with hands-on tasks including painting, general maintenance, light repair work and cleaning. The district is also seeking donations of landscaping items, paint, building supplies and materials. Cash donations to purchase these items would also be appreciated.

If your company is willing to be a sponsor or lend support to this event in any way, please contact the Extreme School Makeover Office with the Independence School District at 816-521-5502 or email extremeinfo@indep.k12.mo.us. If you are able to contribute funds, please make checks for monetary donations payable to The School District of Independence Foundation, Inc. and mail to Extreme School Makeover, 3225 S. Noland Rd, Independence, MO 64055. Contact your tax advisor regarding the deductibility of your cash donation.

The momentum for change is in full force and the Independence School District welcomes your support in inspiring greatness throughout our community.

Sugar Creek, located adjacent to Independence, is a close-knit community of about 4,000 residents. Its proud citizens rallied to support the Independence School District because they believed annexing schools from the Kansas City School District would improve local schools and economic conditions.

See page 6 inside for

2008 SLAVIC FEST

information

Sugar Creek Sweet Talk

Newsletter for Sugar Creek, Missouri • June 2008

Sweet Talk is published monthly by the office of the City Clerk of Sugar Creek, MO at 103 South Sterling, Sugar Creek, MO 64054. For more information call Jana Olivarez-Dickerson at 252-4400, ext. 128 or visit Sugar Creek on the web at www.sugar-creek.mo.us

SUGAR CREEK
ELECTED OFFICIALS

Mayor
  Stanley J. Salva

Aldermen
  Dennis R. Onka
  Stanley J. Sagehorn
  Joseph D. Kenney
  Patrick C. Casey

City Marshal
  Herbert M. Soule

City Administrator
  Ron Martinovich

City Clerk
  Jana Olivarez-Dickerson

City Treasurer
  Linda Martinovich

City Engineer
  Elizabeth Arasmith

Building Official
  Paul Loving

Director of
Public Works
  Ed Layton

Parks & Recreation
Supervisor
  Sue Mikula

City Attorney
  C. Robert Buckley

Municipal Judge
  Garry L. Helm

Municipal Court Clerk
  Donna Newton

Povala Sisters Named Family Of The Year

Sugar Creek natives Joan Kolich and Maryagnes Onka, the "Povala Sisters," have been named 2007 Family of the Year.

The sisters were honored by the Mayor and Board of Aldermen for their accomplishments and contributions to their children, their church, and to their community, and especially their on-going daily example of the meaning of family. AppleMarket on 24Hwy and Sterling donated a $50.00 gift card to the Family of the Year.

"We were very surprised and awed by it all," said Joan, the older of the two. "It was a wonderful surprise."

She said that while growing up in Sugar Creek, they felt very safe and were fortunate to live in a community where they could travel all over town on their own during the day.

They were always surrounded by the Mayors of Sugar Creek. Though they had no brothers while growing up at 210. N. Sterling, they

Joan Kolich and Maryagnes Onka, better known as the "Povala Sisters" were named as Sugar Creek's 2007 Family of the Year.

played croquet, kick the can and baseball all the time with Charles Dumsky and Jack O'Renick, and Rudy Roper was their neighbor and Stanley Salva current Mayor lived across the street.

"We felt very honored," added Maryagnes. "I couldn't want to live in a sweeter place." To this day, she feels safe and fortunate to live

in Sugar Creek. "I've lived other places, but there is no place like home."

"We both wondered why we were chosen," she continued, but were thankful for the nomination.

The sisters went to school through the ninth grade in Sugar Creek and
— please see "The Povala Sisters" on page 4

School Makeovers Will Need Volunteers

The Independence School District is gearing up for the 2008-2009 school year. Volunteers are needed for the Extreme School Makeover Weekend, happening this summer. The planned dates are July 26 and 27. The Makeover Weekend is an event to revitalize the school buildings acquired in western Independence and Sugar Creek and prepare them for students returning this fall as students of the Independence School District.

Volunteers and supplies are needed in order for the Extreme School Makeover to be a successful event.

EXTREME SCHOOL MAKEOVER
Get Involved.

★　★　★　★　★

The district is seeking donations of landscaping items, paint, building supplies and materials. Cash donations to purchase these items would also be appreciated. If you and/or your company are willing to be a donor or a major sponsor of this event, please contact the Extreme School Makeover office.

If you have any questions or are interested in volunteering or sponsorship opportunities, please phone the Extreme School Makeover information line at 816-521-5502 or email extremei-
— please see "School Makeovers" on page 4

Nearly 3,000 volunteers turned out to work from dawn to dusk during the swelter-ing hot Extreme School Makeover weekend of July 26-27, 2008. Individuals and families in all walks of life showed up to pitch in, some of them arriving with picks, shovels, hammers, nails, cleaning materials, and gardening supplies.

Extreme Makeover is about schools, students

The Examiner/AMY ELROD

Operative Plasterers and Cement Masons 518's, from left, Joe Hill, Brian Ran-dle, Butch Pekarek, and Jim Renick, poor and smooth new concrete outside of Van Horn High School. The concrete was donated by Fordyce and Lafarge to continue the effort of the Independence school makeover.

▶MAKEOVER | From A1

believe the work ethic they had and their willingness to do whatever we needed," said Jean Carton, principal at Nowlin Middle School. "Things are so bright and shiny now. We have teachers moving into their classrooms and going through materials. It simply looks like a new building."

Duran, who was the project foreman at Three Trails Ele-mentary, said by the end of the weekend, more than 100 gal-lons of paint had been used on the interior with an another 30 gallons used outside.

In addition, windows were replaced, doors and class-rooms were painted and the parking lot was restriped. He said the outside and the inside of Three Trails now look "pristine."

"I have a belief that better students make better citi-zens," he said. "After it was all completed, I was a little sore, but I have this huge sense of accomplishment. Students will be showing up there in two weeks and are going to have a much cleaner learning environment. It is brighter and more appealing so those kids can go learn things."

Earl Williamson, leader of a Maywood Baptist Church group, said his reason for vol-unteering was simple – "it was all for the kids."

He said by Saturday morn-

ing of Extreme School Makeover, the number of vol-unteers from Maywood Bap-tist had risen by more than 100, topping out at 350. Williamson said he was excit-ed about the opportunity to make a difference in the lives of the children.

"I think this is good not only for the kids in western Independence, but also for the teachers who will be teaching in the Independence School District. It is a blessing and encouraging for them," he said. "We had the whole build-ing painted by Sunday night. I felt relieved when it was done and wonderful because although we were tired, we had a good time and worked hard."

Carton said she was moved by all the assistance from the community.

She said from the paint to the overall cleanliness of the buildings, the transforma-

tions are "incredible."

"I believe the new coat of paint on the walls is symbol-ic," she said. "It is a new way and a new day in the for our children in the Independence School District."

> They were phenomenal. I just couldn't believe the work ethic they had...
>
> JEAN CARTON
> Nowlin Middle School Principal

Article courtesy of *The Examiner.*

Making an eXtReMe difference in student's lives

The Examiner/AMY ELROD

Butch Pekarek, right, and Brian Randle guide concrete as it is poured on a newly resurfaced sidewalk outside of Van Horn High School in Indepen-dence.

By KELLY EVENSON
kelly.evenson@examiner.net

When Tony Duran walked into Three Trails Elementary two weeks ago, he could only describe it as a mess.

Graffiti was on the walls, there was no striping on the parking lots, basketball courts and the running track had not been maintained in years, and the whole build-ing was in desperate need of a fresh coat of paint.

"Someone has to do it," said Duran after being asked why he wanted to be involved in the renovation efforts. "The way I looked at it was that it needed to be done, so I was going to help."

MAKING A DIFFERENCE

Extreme School Makeover Volunteers

Duran was one of the more than 2,500 vol-unteers who participated in Extreme School Makeover last month. The event, organized by the Independence School District, was an effort to revitalize and refresh six buildings that entered the Independence School District this summer in a transfer from the Kansas City School District. Voters approved the boundary change last November.

Independence officials are planning a recognition cele-bration to honor those volun-teers that spent two days paint-ing, cleaning and landscaping the facilities.

"They were phenomenal. I just couldn't See MAKEOVER / **A3**

Article courtesy of *The Examiner.*

Independence School District Superintendent Dr. Jim Hinson, Missouri State Senator Victor Callahan, attorney Steve Mauer and Pastor Bob Spradling were honored as "Citizens of the Year" in September 2008 for their devoted and successful leadership during the school district's boundary change initiative.

Citizens of the Year announced

2008 Honorees

INDEPENDENCE
Superintendent Jim Hinson
State Senator Victor Callahan
Attorney Steve Mauer
The Rev. Bob Spradling

SUGAR CREEK
Attorney Bob and Ellen Welch

BLUE SPRINGS
Mark and Cheryl Mozer

LEE'S SUMMIT   **RAYTOWN**
Geneva High   Mike Apprill

GRAIN VALLEY   **OAK GROVE**
Mary Strack   Norby Corn

KANSAS CITY
The Rev. John Modest Miles

LAKE WINNEBAGO
David Claycomb

The Examiner/JULIE SCHEIDEGGER

Independence School District superintendent Dr. Jim Hinson stands outside of North Rock Creek/Korte Academy School to give a press conference concerning the exchange of eight buildings from the Kansas City School District to the Independence School District on July 1, 2008.

By THE EXAMINER STAFF

A family that helps fight cancer, a community volunteer, and the team behind the transfer of seven schools from the Kansas City to Independence School District are some of the honorees as Citizens of the Year.

The annual awards are presented by the Truman Heartland Community Foundation at its Toast of the Towns Gala, which will be Sept. 20 at the Hyatt Regency Hotel in Kansas City. Qualifications include a commitment to charitable giving and improving area communities by promoting private giving for the public good.

Citizens from nine communities, as selected by mayors of those cities, will be honored at the event along with the "Heartland Humanitarian of the Year Award" to Larry Moore of KMBC 9 News and the "Corporate Citizen of the Year Award" to Vicki Digby of MeraVic.

Four members of the school transition team will receive the honor for Independence. Superintendent Jim Hinson, State Sen. Victor Callahan, attorney Steve Mauer and the Rev. Bob Spradling will be honored for their support during the election and transfer process. The four were instrumental in getting seven schools in western Independence and Sugar Creek removed from the Kansas City School District and added to the Independence School District.

Legislation introduced by Callahan helped make the transfer possible, then voters in both school districts approved the transfer after citizens gathered signatures to put in the ballot. After more legal hurdles were cleared this summer, and a massive community effort to help renovate the buildings, school will open

See CITIZENS / **A3**

The 2008 Citizens of the Year

▶ CITIZENS I From A1

later this month on time and with renewed hope for students in western Independence and Sugar Creek.

Sugar Creek's Citizens of the Year are attorney Bob and Ellen "Jake" Welch, who have been active philanthropists in the Sugar Creek for more than 40 years, giving to area bar associations, bar & law foundations, and the City's Parks and Recreation Department.

In Blue Springs, the winners are Mark and Cheryl Mozer, who have advocated both in Washington, D.C. and in Kansas City for funding for childhood cancer. The Mozers have spearheaded Alex's Lemonade Stands fundraisers in Kansas City raising more than $300,000 for cancer research.

Other honorees:

■ Lee's Summit – Geneva High.

Having served in many capacities throughout the city of Lee's Summit and receiving many awards for her contribu-

tions, High is perhaps most known for her service as executive director of Lee's Summit Social Services, where she has remained since its formation in 1992.

■ Raytown – Mike Apprill.

Retired from Aquila in 2006 as vice-president of wholesale marketing, Apprill has been an active community member and volunteer in Raytown. He has provided support to Raytown Emergency Assistance Program, United Way, Raytown Optimists, Raytown Shepherd's Center and many others.

■ Grain Valley – Mary Strack.

Strack has been very involved in the Grain Valley community by volunteering her time to the work of the Historical Society, school district, Christian Church, Community Services League and the Grain Valley Assistance Council.

■ Oak Grove – Norby Corn.

The owner of the Apple Market in Oak Grove, Corn has provided charitable support to countless area nonprofits, sports teams, school-sponsored

organizations and scouting programs since 1980.

■ Kansas City – The Rev. John Modest Miles.

Miles serves as pastor at Morning Star Baptist Church for the last 21 years and has also served on many community-based boards and been recognized for his dedication to the community and the City of Kansas City.

■ Lake Winnebago – David Claycomb.

Co-founder and executive vice president of BioStar Systems, Claycomb serves on the St. Joseph Hospital Foundation and Blue Valley Industries, and has been active in the Lee's Summit Chamber of Commerce and is small cities representative to the Cass County Economic Development Corporation.

THCF continues to serve the region with assets reaching $35 million and annual grants surpassing $3 million. For more information abouty the gala or charitable giving, visit www.thcf.org or call the office at 816-836-8189.

Article courtesy of *The Examiner.*

Hundreds of Independence and Sugar Creek residents volunteered to help renovate Roper Stadium and the public park that surrounds it in a "Mini-Makeover" on March 22, 2009. The event was coordinated by the Independence School District to preserve the civic initiative that started with the Extreme School Makeover of 2008.

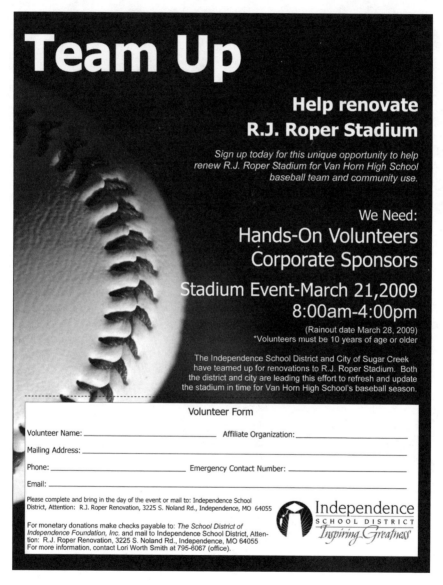

In May 2009, residents welcomed back their native son Rick Sutcliffe, a 1974 Van Horn High School grad who won Rookie of the Year pitching for the Los Angeles Dodgers and the Cy Young Award with the Chicago Cubs. Sutcliffe told kids that Major League Baseball scouts years earlier were as interested in his grade point average as his fastball.

FREE ADMISSION

RICK SUTCLIFFE DAY
Thursday, May 7, 2009
VAN HORN HIGH SCHOOL vs. ST. MARY'S HIGH SCHOOL
at R.J. Roper Stadium (131 S. Carlisle Ave, Sugar Creek, MO 64054)

Celebrate with VHHS alumni, coaches, teachers and players!

RICK SUTCLIFFE is a 1974 Van Horn High School graduate where he was an All-State and All-American athlete in baseball, football and basketball. In 1974, Rick began his career by being drafted by the LA Dodgers in the first round. His 19-year span in the Majors includes eight years with the Chicago Cubs and several highlights and awards, comprising Rookie of the Year, three-time All-Star, Cy Young Award and the United States Junior Chamber Ten Outstanding Young Americans Award. Since 2002, Rick has been working as an ESPN television sportscaster (Wednesday game of the week).

SCHEDULE FOR THE EVENING

5:00PM **Rick Sutcliffe** addresses players and community

5:30PM *Pitching Clinic for VHHS and SMHS players*

6:30PM OPENING CEREMONY
Retiring of the #17 jersey presented by Independence School District

Comments by Senator Victor Callahan

Outstanding Missourian Award presented by Missouri State Representative Ray Salva

Street Dedication presented by the City of Sugar Creek

7:15PM GAME TIME
Play-by-play with KC radio legend David Lawrence, Missouri State Representative Ray Salva and VHHS alum Fred Coats

Rain out date Friday, May 8, 2009

Enter the raffle to win signed sports memorabilia from various pro-athletes.

PRESENTED BY:

Van Horn High School
Booster Club

Independence
SCHOOL DISTRICT
Inspiring Greatness
THE SUTCLIFFE FOUNDATION

Sugar
Creek
MISSOURI

The weekend of July 18, 2009, Independence and Sugar Creek citizens again enthusiastically partnered with the Independence School District. More than 1,000 volunteers joined "Project Shine" to spruce up five schools, including three acquired in the annexation. Plans are for Project Shine to be an annual event.

When schools gleam, kids beam.

Call the Project Shine hotline at 816.521.5502
or go to OurSchoolsShine.org to register

July 18/19

The momentum of positive change that began with Extreme School Makeover continues with Project Shine. One weekend, every year, the Independence School District will lead volunteer-based projects at designated schools to clean, paint and update. Together, we can make our community shine!

2009 Project Shine schools: Chrisman, Van Horn, Bridger, Nowlin, Korte

Project Shine Event* - July 18, 8am - 5pm and July 19, 1pm - 5pm
We Need: Hands-On Volunteers** • Supplies • Corporate Sponsors

Monetary Donations: Make checks payable to: The School District of Independence Foundation, Inc. and mail to Project Shine, 3225 S. Noland Rd., Independence, MO 64055, or visit OurSchoolsShine.org

*Rain or Shine
** Volunteer all day or anytime during event hours.
Volunteers must be 16 years of age or older.

Independence
SCHOOL DISTRICT
Inspiring Greatness

5/09

Dr. Jim Hinson, with Sandi Kiehne, Assistant Superintendent-Educational Programs, Jana Waits of the Independence School District Board of Education, and Blake Roberson, President of the Board of Education, accepts the "Distinction in Performance" accreditation for the district, which earned the state distinction in 2006, 2007, 2008 and 2009.

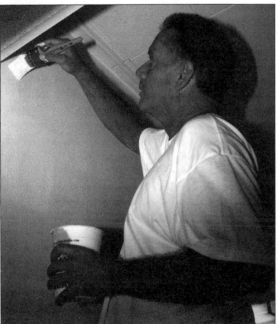

America's Promise Alliance: www.americaspromise.org

American Bar Association Division for Public Education:
www.abanet.org/publiced

American Association of Colleges for Teacher Education:
www.aacte.org

American Association of School Administrators: www.aasa.org

American Association of School Personnel Administrators:
www.aaspa.org

American Federation of Teachers: www.aaspa.org

American School Counselor Association: www.schoolcounselor.org

Association of School Business Officials International:
www.asbointl.org

Annenberg Institute for School Reform: www.annenberginstitute.org

Cato Institute: www.cato.org

**Center for Educational Innovation—Public
Education Association:** www.cei-pea.org

Center for Law and Education: www.cleweb.org

Charis Community Housing: www.chariscommunity.org

Coalition for Community Schools: www.communityschools.org

Council of Chief State School Officers: www.ccsso.org

**Edward Zigler Center in Child Development and
Social Policy:** www.ziglercenter.yale.edu

FCS Urban Ministries: www.FCSMinistries.org

Harry S. Truman Library & Museum: www.trumanlibrary.org

Independence School District: www6.indep.k12.mo.us

Learning First Alliance: www.publicschoolinsights.org/about

Local Investment Commission: www.kclinc.org

Missouri Association of School Administrators:
www.masaonline.org

**Missouri Department of Elementary and
Secondary Education:** dese.mo.gov

National Association of Elementary School Principals:
www.naesp.org

National Association of School Psychologists: www.nasponline.org

National Association of Secondary School Principals:
www.principals.org

National Association of State Boards of Education: www.nasbe.org

**National Association of State Directors of
Special Education:** www.nasdse.org

National Coalition for Parent Involvement in Education:
www.ncpie.org

National Community Education Association: www.ncea.com

National Education Association: www.nea.org

NEA Foundation: www.neafoundation.org

National Middle School Association: www.nmsa.org

National Parent Teacher Association: www.pta.org

National Staff Development Council: www.nsdc.org

National School Boards Association: www.nsba.org

National School Public Relations Association: www.nspra.org

Northwest Communities Development Corporation:
www.nwcdc-mo.org

Phi Delta Kappa International: www.pdkintl.org

Public Education Network: www.publiceducation.org

U.S. Department of Education: www.ed.gov

University City Children's Center: www.uccc.org

Yale Prevention Research Center: www.davidkatzmd.com

Publisher's Note

*The involvement of the faith-based communities of Western Indepen-
dence was significant throughout the annexation process and played an
integral role in the success of the Independence School District boundary change. A factually accurate account of the events that transpired
throughout the annexation process cannot be accomplished without de-
scribing the involvement of the faith-based communities and factors that
contributed to their drive and determination. Any reference in this book
to religion, religious faith, religious analogies, or religious resources
does not reflect or represent the position or beliefs of the Independence
School District. Any involvement by Independence School District employees or board members in religious-based activities described in this
book was made in their individual capacities and not in their capacity
as an employee or official of the school district.*